EXPLORING
Machine Trapunto
NEW DIMENSIONS

Hari Walner

C&T PUBLISHING

©1999 Hari Walner
Illustrations ©1999 Hari Walner

Editor: Liz Aneloski
Technical Editor: Sara Kate MacFarland
Copy Editor: Vera Tobin
Front Cover Designer: Micaela Miranda Carr
Back Cover Designer: Aliza Kahn
Book Designer: Rose Sheifer
Design Director: Diane Pedersen
Quilt photography: Brian Birlauf, Denver, Colorado
Studio photography: Dan Looper Photography, Loveland, Colorado
Author photo: Courtesy of Hari Walner
Illustrations: Hari Walner
Published by C&T Publishing, Inc., P.O. Box 1456, Lafayette, California 94549

Attention Teachers:
C&T Publishing, Inc. encourages you to use this book as a text for teaching. Contact us at 800-284-1114 or www.ctpub.com for more information about the C&T Teachers Program.

We take great care to ensure that the information included in this book is accurate and presented in good faith, but no warranty is provided nor results guaranteed. Since we have no control over the choice of materials or procedures used, neither the author nor C&T Publishing, Inc. shall have any liability to any person or entity with respect to any loss or damage caused directly or indirectly by the information contained in this book.

Trademarked (™) and Registered Trademarked (®) names are used throughout this book. Rather than use the symbols with every occurance of a trademark and registered trademark name, we are using the names only in an editorial fashion and to the benefit of the owner, with no intention of infringement.

Library of Congress Cataloging-in-Publication Data

Walner, Hari
        Exploring machine trapunto : new dimensions / Hari Walner.
                    p.   cm.
        Includes index.
        ISBN 1-57120-043-6 (pbk.)
        1. Trapunto—Patterns. 2. Machine quilting—Patterns. I. Title.
TT835.W3563 1999
746.46—dc21   98-4491
                                                                  CIP

Printed in Hong Kong
10 9 8 7 6 5 4 3 2 1

CONTENTS

This book is for

Gordon Snow, my lifemate and business partner. . . for his constant and ongoing encouragement, help, and beautiful smiles and hugs.

Thank you to

. . . special quilter friends who helped with last minute quiltmaking and finishing tasks: Cheryl Osborn, Ramona Hilton, Sue Danielson, Cheryl Phillips, Linda Taylor, and Alice Wilhoit. I am very grateful for their support and unique applied friendships.

. . . the many wonderful quilters in the Nebraska State Quilt Guild and others who, with beautiful sharing spirits, came to my rescue with fabrics to complete the cover quilt.

. . . C&T Publishing for the patience and understanding they have shown when events of life did not agree with the publishing deadlines I had agreed to. A note of warm gratitude to editor Liz Aneloski and production director Diane Pedersen for keeping a cheerful attitude throughout my whining.

Freda's Star, 94" x 94"
Hari Walner

Freda Remer Steiger, my grandmother, pieced this quilt top for her grandson, Pete Allen, sometime in the late 1940s. It had been sitting on a shelf for almost fifty years when my aunt Beverly gave it to me a few years ago. I added the two borders.

Because many of the original fabrics were fragile, I inserted good quality muslin between the quilt top and the trapunto batting. To take up slack in the distorted star patches, I added a trapunto batting behind the entire pieced star as well as behind the quilting motifs. I used a quilting machine so I could attach this huge trapunto batting without further damaging the fabrics. I'm not sure these old, weak fabrics would have withstood the extreme handling of quilting on a regular sewing machine. The quilt is now stable and heavily quilted and will be passed on in our family.

The poem I wrote for the border is rendered with cornerstone quilting as explained in Idea Two (page 30). The quilting inside the lettering consists of parallel lines stitched closely together. The pieced star pattern is repeated for the quilting design as suggested in Idea One (page 28). Between each star point is a one-eighth section of the Zenith design, shown on page 82.

The Category is Quilts,
19'' x 15''
Hari Walner

This book is about reaching out and exploring trapunto techniques that can be used to add another dimension to your quilting.

- The book begins with the Pictorial Glossary—an easy visual reference for terms and techniques used in this book.
- The Basics chapter gives lessons in free-motion quilting, machine trapunto, and basting. Also included are tips to help hand quilters use this trapunto technique.
- There are seven ideas in The Ideas chapter, each suggesting another way to explore this trapunto method. Many of the techniques involve the use of water-soluble basting thread.
- Thirty-one new, original quilting patterns, all suitable for machine trapunto, were designed just for this book. They appear in The Designs chapter.
- Photographs of quilts throughout the book show what many talented quilters have done with these new designs.
- Near the end of the book is an an Easy-Find Design Index that allows you to compare the designs and to make it easy to locate each design quickly.

Because this book explores techniques, there are no piecing directions for the quilts shown. However, I have included as much information as possible, including measurements, sources, and so forth.

My goal in writing this book is to share information that might inspire you to take these concepts to your own, higher level of creativity. Please experiment with and explore these ideas in your quilting.

GLOSSARY

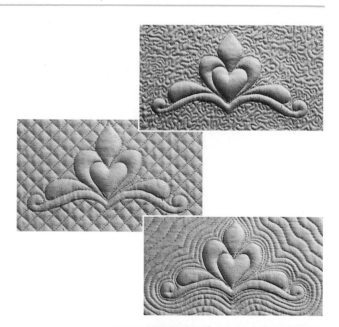

Background Quilting

Background quilting stitches compact the batting in the areas immediately surrounding a quilting design to accent the design and make it stand out. Many quilting styles can be used, including, but not limited to, the styles shown: stipple (tight meandering) quilting, grid quilting, and echo quilting.

Backtracking

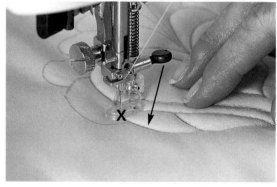

Backtracking is the technique of stitching back on top of previous stitches. It can be expedient when machine quilting a pattern that is not designed with one continuous line. When stitching over stitches that are already in place, keep your eye on the next four to six stitches you are about to stitch back over. Do not watch the needle on your machine. In this book, any backtracking you might need to do to complete a design is pointed out in the directional diagram.

Basting the Trapunto Batting

This is the method of attaching the trapunto batting onto the back of the quilt top with water-soluble basting thread to achieve the "stuffed" effect (see page 18). This is done before the quilt sandwich is layered and basted (see next definition).

Basting the Quilt Sandwich

The process of securing the layers of your quilt (quilt top, batting, and backing) to prevent the layers from shifting and slipping while you are quilting (see page 22).

Batting

Batting is usually used for the middle layer of a quilt sandwich. In these trapunto techniques, different battings serve different purposes.

Trapunto Batting —This is the thick batting used to achieve the "stuffed" effect. It is basted onto your quilt before the quilt sandwich is made (see pages 6 and 18). It can be very thick polyester batting or several layers of cotton batting.

Regular Batting—This is the overall batting used to make the quilt sandwich.

Cording

The term cording is used to denote the effect of using a narrow strip of extra batting to give the impression of a thick cording raising the image. There are three simulated cording techniques presented in this book (see pages 32-35).

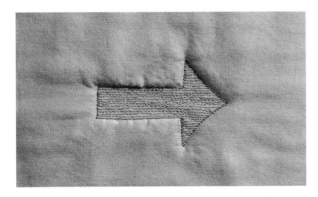

Cornerstone Quilting

A reversed trapunto technique; "stuffing" the surrounding area and compacting the design motif makes the motif appear indented. This quilting is reminiscent of the designs often seen in the cornerstones of buildings and headstones (see pages 30-31).

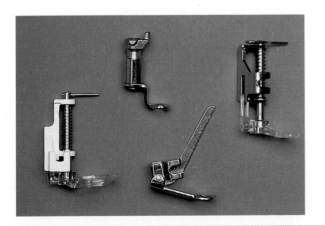

Darning Foot

A darning foot is an accessory for the sewing machine used for free-motion quilting. This foot's purpose is to hold the fabric layers down while the needle is in the fabric so your machine can make a nice stitch. The foot lifts up from the fabric when the needle raises. This allows you to control the movement of your quilt. There is a wide variety of darning feet available. Look for a darning foot that lets you see the design area around the foot easily.

GLOSSARY

Feed Dogs (also called Feed Teeth)

These are small serrated teeth that protrude through the throat plate of your sewing machine. In normal stitching, these teeth help move the fabric along and determine the stitch length. When free-motion quilting, feed dogs are always lowered or covered so they cannot inhibit the way you move the quilt.

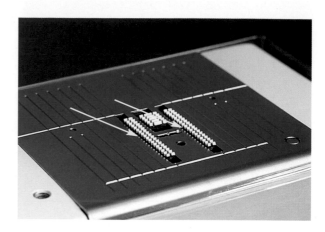

Free-Motion Quilting

Free-motion machine quilting is done in a manner that allows you to move your quilt from side-to-side and front-to-back while you are stitching. It is easiest to do with a darning or free-motion quilting foot and with your feed dogs lowered so they do not inhibit the movement of your quilt. See pages 13-16 for details on how to free-motion quilt.

Machine Trapunto

Machine trapunto is used to achieve the "stuffed" effect (trapunto) with your sewing machine without making holes in the back of your quilt. This technique was developed for machine quilters, but can also be used by hand quilters. See pages 17-21 for details on the basic machine trapunto technique and its refinements.

Back of Quilt

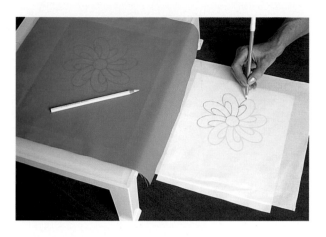

Marking

There are several methods you can use to copy or draw the quilting design onto your quilt, so you have a guide when quilting. If you have a light, solid-colored fabric, you can simply lay the fabric on top of the design and trace it. If the fabric is dark or the design is faint, you can use a light box underneath the design and the fabric or tape the design and fabric to a window and trace the design.

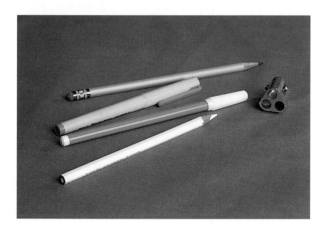

Marking Tools

Pencils, pens, chalk marking devices, and many other tools can be used to mark the quilting images onto your fabric. Select a tool that makes the marks easy to see and also easy to remove. For machine quilting, it is important to see your marks clearly. Always test on a scrap of the exact fabric you are going to use to be sure the marks can be removed. Follow the manufacturer's instructions.

Needles

Use the type and size of needle that works best with the thread you have chosen. This can vary from stitcher to stitcher and from machine to machine. The needles that work well for me are:

For regular free-motion quilting, with 50-weight machine embroidery thread: jeans/denim needle, size 70. It you are just beginning to free-motion quilt, you may like a size 80.

For basting the trapunto batting with water-soluble thread: machine embroidery needles, size 75 or 90. My choice depends on the thickness of the trapunto batting. When I use extra-thick batting, I always use size 90.

For quilting with exotic or temperamental threads: machine embroidery needles size 75 or 90. The size depends on whether or not the thread has a tendency to break. If it does, I use the larger, size 90 needle.

For straight-line quilting with machine quilting thread: jeans/denim needle, size 80.

Quilt Sandwich

The three layers of a quilt: the quilt top, the batting, and the backing. These three layers are then basted securely together before the final quilting begins.

Shadow Trapunto

This technique uses only one piece of fabric for the quilted area on the quilt top, but gives the illusion that more than one fabric was used. It is achieved by using a slightly transparent fabric (lawn cotton or batiste-type fabric), cotton batting, and a bright fabric on top of the regular batting when basting the quilt sandwich. The bright fabric shows through the translucent fabric, but not through the trapunto batting.

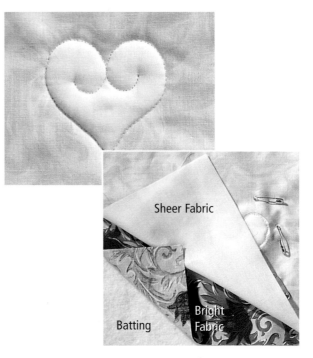

Shading Stitches

These are short lines of secondary quilting stitches used to create detail within a quilting design. They are added at the same time you stitch along a primary line of the design. These lines are usually only five to ten stitches long and require backtracking to get back to the longer, primary line. Although shading stitches enhance the detail and depth of the design, they can be omitted and the design will still be complete.

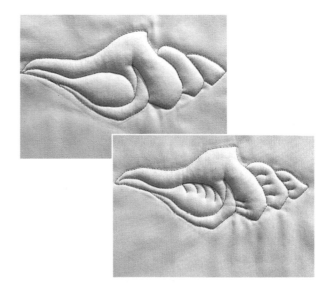

Straight-Line Quilting

Straight-line quilting refers to lines of straight stitches made using a walking foot (your regular presser foot will do) with the feed dogs up. Straight-line quilting is used for quilting along seamlines (in-the-ditch) and in a grid pattern. On a bed quilt, the thread used for straight lines of quilting stitches is the most vulnerable to breaking, so use a stronger thread when quilting straight lines than when doing free-motion (curved) quilting.

Thread

There are thousands of acceptable threads. Three considerations come into play when deciding which thread to use. For best results, all three should be satisfied.

1. The intended use
2. Your personal sense of aesthetics
3. Availability

Machine Quilting Thread—For straight-line quilting I use 30-weight or equivalent thread.

Machine Embroidery Thread—With the exception of when I use exotic threads for special effects, I generally use 50-weight for free-motion quilting.

Water-Soluble Basting Thread—This thread is made to dissolve in water. It is used for basting the trapunto batting to the quilt top and for basting smaller quilts. Several brands are available. Lighter-weight threads seem to work fine in dry climates, while the heavier-weight threads might work better in high-humidity areas. Heavier threads take a few minutes longer to dissolve, but they may be the answer for those who have breakage problems with the lighter threads. Beware of threads that don't dissolve. Test before using it on your quilt.

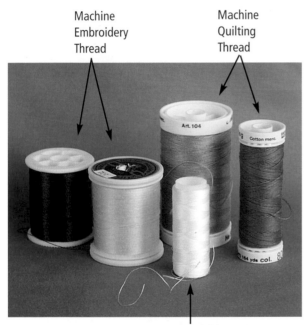

Machine Embroidery Thread

Machine Quilting Thread

Water-soluble BastingThread

Walking Foot
(also called an Even-Feed Foot)

A walking foot has feed dogs on the foot that work in tandem with the movement of the needle. It is useful when stitching straight lines and very gentle curves and is helpful when stitching thick or bulky fabric. It is also useful when sewing layers of fabric together, because the feed dogs of the walking foot work with the feed dogs under the needle to gently move the layers of fabric. This helps to prevent unwanted puckering and pleating.

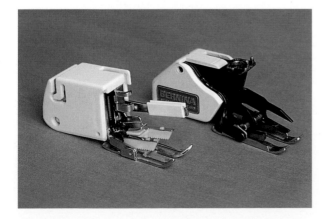

THE BASICS

Machine Quilted,
17'' x 15''
Hari Walner
Quilting pattern
on page 96.

This section will explain and demonstrate the skills needed to pursue the Ideas in this book (see pages 27-46). It is written to be easily understood by a beginning machine quilter, but there are tips included that may be of use to those of you with more experience as well. Check the Pictorial Glossary (pages 6-11) for hints about needles, thread, marking tools, darning feet, etc.

- Free-Motion Quilting
  A guide to learning and enjoying this wonderful skill

- Machine Trapunto
  A simple method and some new refinements to achieve an elegant trapunto effect

- Hand Quilting Using This Trapunto Method
  Only the hand quilting shows

- Basting for Beauty
  Baste it well for beautiful quilting

Free-Motion Machine Quilting

● You need a flat surface for your quilt to rest on when you machine quilt. Situate your sewing machine cabinet or an extension table so the throat plate of the machine is level with the surrounding surface.

● Your quilt must be very easy to maneuver on the flat surface. If it slips off the edge of the surface it will tug at your needle. If you fight this tug instead of finding a remedy, frustration sets in rapidly. Broken needles are one side effect of not having a good working surface. It is extremely difficult to free-motion quilt on just the free-arm of a sewing machine.

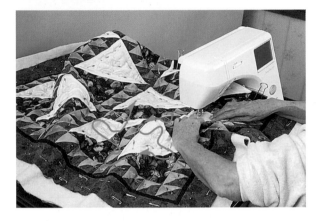

● Make sure your lighting is adequate. The small light on your sewing machine is not enough. You are not being fair to yourself if you stitch in a dim light and then examine your work in a bright light. (For happy quilting, do it the other way around—stitch in a bright light and examine it in a dim light.)

Use a chair that fits you well and that you are comfortable getting in and out of. If it is difficult to "get up" from your chair, you will not take enough breaks from your quilting.

● Put on music that makes you feel relaxed and quietly inspired.

Free-motion quilting is a term used for machine quilting with the feed dogs down and a darning foot attached. This combination allows you to move your quilt in any direction; front-to-back, back-to-front, and side-to-side. This freedom of movement allows you to stitch beautiful, intricate designs.

Now, we will go through the process, step-by-step. This demonstration will use Shell We Quilt? (page 78) for a quilting pattern.

Prepare the Quilt

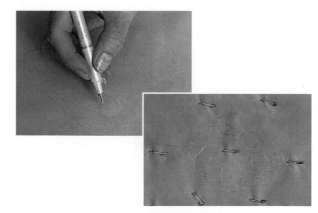

1 Trace the design onto a 12" x 12" piece of muslin with your marking tool.

Layer this marked quilt top with a piece of batting (cotton or cotton blend is easiest to begin with) and a piece of fabric for the backing. Baste well. Try not to put pins in the path where you will be stitching.

Prepare the Machine

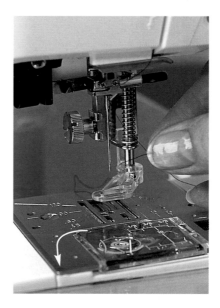

2 Thread your needle and fill your bobbin with a thread that you would like to stitch with. If you are new to machine quilting, use a good grade, lightweight cotton. Machine embroidery thread (50 weight) is good to start with.

Lower the feed dogs. If you cannot lower the feed dogs on your machine, cover them. There is usually a small plastic cover in the accessory box for machines that don't have this feature. This cover will snap into place over the feed dogs. The idea is to render them inactive and out of the way.

Attach a darning foot to your machine.

Get Ready. . .

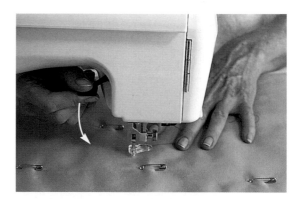

3 Slide your quilt sandwich under the needle to the area where you want to begin stitching.

Lower the presser foot lever to engage the top thread tension. If you forget to lower the presser foot lever, you will get long loops on the *underside* of your quilt. (I call this fringe quilting.)

Pull the bobbin thread to the surface by holding the needle thread, turning the wheel one full rotation, and giving a little tug on the thread. The bobbin thread should always be on top when you begin quilting.

Fringe Quilting

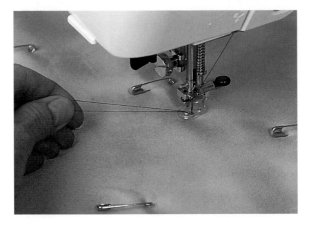

Begin Stitching

4 To make a knot, slowly begin stitching and take seven to ten very short stitches right next to each other, along the line of the design. In order to do this you have to move your quilt very slowly. Don't forget, the feed dogs are down and there is no machine control over the stitch length. These tiny stitches will make a secure knot. Do not stitch in place or you will have a little nub on the back of your quilt.

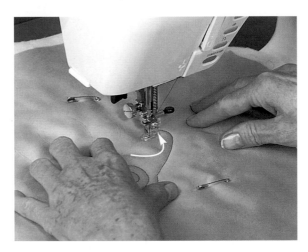

5 Now, think of feeding the line of the design into the needle. Do not watch your needle*. Watch the design line you are feeding into the needle. Look "down-the-road" 1/4''–1/2''. Move your quilt front-to-back, side-to-side, and back-to-front, as the design dictates.

Stitch at a comfortable speed. If you try to make yourself go faster or slower than your comfort level allows, you will not keep a steady pace. It is the steady, smooth stitching that keeps your stitches even and your mind quiet. I encourage you to stitch at a pace comfortable for you.

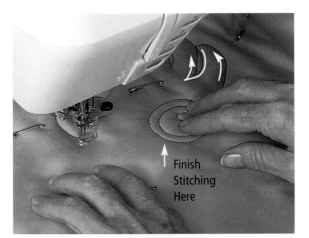

Finish Stitching Here

6 Continue stitching in this free-motion manner. If this is new to you, you may feel a little light-headed because it seems like you are out of control. Relax, you will soon realize that you are in control.

Keep the quilt oriented the same way. Try not to turn it. It is easy to stop and turn a small quilt, but it is impossible to turn a large quilt in the machine. Teach yourself not to turn the quilt. You will be glad you did.

When you are about an 1/8'' from the end of the line of the design, begin taking very short stitches right next to each other to secure the stitches. Make these tiny stitches to the end of the design line.

*THINK ABOUT THIS
No matter how hard you stare at your needle, it is going to continue to go up and down in the same little hole. The needle never moves laterally. What is moving, and what you have control over, is your quilt. Look at the line of your design while stitching.

Whoops! I Made A Mistake...

...or did you? Don't be too quick to judge yourself in this matter. Sometimes you only drift off the line of your design a little bit. Don't let your mind's eye exaggerate this. The line rinses out. No one, not even you, will ever know.

Yes, there will be times when you make mistakes you want to remedy. Try this fix.

1 Immediately stop stitching. Do not make a knot to secure the threads. Raise your needle and lift the presser foot lever to release the upper thread tension.

2 Carefully slide your quilt under the needle to the area on your quilt 1/4'' before your stitches went awry.

3 Lower your needle into a perfectly good stitch. Now, make a secure knot by taking those tiny stitches right on top of the good stitches, along the direction you want to stitch. By making the tiny stitches on top of the good stitches, you have locked off the old line and, at the same time, locked on the new line. Continue stitching.

When you have finished your quilting session, take your seam ripper and lift the errant stitches. Don't forget the threads on the back of your quilt. To help you remember, make caution flags. See TIP.

Later on...

TIP
CAUTION FLAGS
To make "caution" flags, knot a short piece of yarn on a dozen 1'' safety pins. Keep them next to your machine. If you make a mistake that you want to be sure to go back and correct, stop and pin one of these flags next to the mistake. The flag will serve as a reminder and a marker. You need a little piece of yarn or the flag will get lost among pins used for basting. If your quilt is mostly red, pick a contrasting color.

Making the Move

When you finish stitching one design and want to move to another design...

1 Make the tiny, short stitches to secure your current stitching. Raise your needle, and lift the presser foot lever to release the upper thread tension.

2 Slide your quilt under the needle until you get to where you want to begin again.

3 Lower your presser foot lever to re-engage the upper thread tension. Make the tiny, short stitches to begin your new line and start stitching the new design.

Later on, when your quilt is not in the machine, you can go back and clip the connecting threads. Don't forget to clip the connecting bobbin threads on the underside.

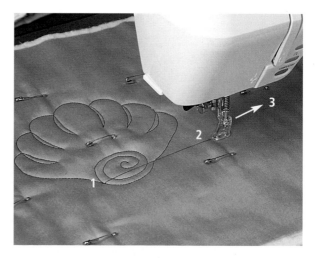

Machine Trapunto

This simple trapunto technique eliminates having to make holes or cuts in the backs of your quilts.

First, a quick word about trapunto and how this technique differs from older, traditional methods. Trapunto is the name given to the techniques that achieve the stuffed look in quilts. In older quilts, this was achieved after all quilting was completed. The techniques that create the trapunto effect in this book are performed *before* the quilting begins.

Materials

Batting

Two different battings are used in this technique.

First, you will need a thick trapunto batting to add loft (puffiness) to the motif. The thickness of the batting you choose determines how puffy the stuffed area will be. You can use a very thick polyester batting or several layers of cotton or cotton-blend batting. Both give excellent results and both have good points and not-so-good points. There is a comparison chart below.

Trapunto Batting

Regular Batting

The second batting is used in the regular manner, as the overall batting you use when making your quilt sandwich. Cotton or cotton-blend batting works best.

Thread

Two different threads are used in this technique (see page 11):
- Water-soluble basting thread (dissolves in water)
- Machine quilting thread

Scissors

Scissors with rounded points work best. My favorites are children's scissors (ages 5-8), pocket scissors, and doctor's bandage scissors. Sharp pointed scissors are not useful for this technique.

Choosing Trapunto Batting

	GOOD	NOT-SO-GOOD
POLYESTER	• Lightweight • Good loft—the thicker the batting the better • Easier to trim than cotton • Dries much faster than cotton	• Can be bulky and hard to handle in the machine • Doesn't give quite the firm feel you get with cotton
SEVERAL LAYERS (USUALLY 3) OF COTTON	• Good loft; very opaque • Slightly firmer feel to the loft	• Extremely difficult to cut all layers at once; easiest to cut one layer at a time; cutting takes much longer • Takes much longer to dry

- Two 12'' squares of muslin or solid, light-colored fabric

- 7'' square of very thick trapunto batting

- 12'' square of cotton batting

- Water-soluble basting thread

- Machine embroidery thread

- Scissors

- Marking tool of your choice

Sparkling Dahlia

For this demonstration we will use the Sparkling Dahlia design. The full-size pattern and directional stitching diagrams are on page 98.

This is a free-motion technique so you will need a darning foot for your sewing machine and to be able to drop or cover your feed dogs.

1 Place your fabric on top of the design and trace the design onto one muslin square. Pin the thick polyester batting to the back of the marked square. Do not use the other piece of fabric at this time.

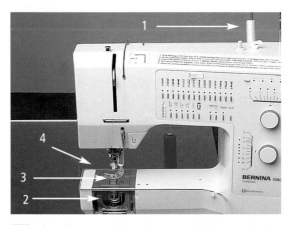

2 Thread your needle with water-soluble thread and fill your bobbin with regular white thread. Drop or cover your feed dogs. Attach a darning foot.

TIP

If your water soluble thread breaks often, try this tip from Janet Finley. Wind the thread onto a bobbin and put the bobbin on the thread holder.

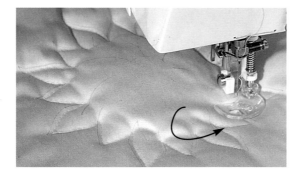

3 Free-motion stitch just ($1/16$'') inside the outline of the design. If your trapunto batting is very thick, you might want to stitch further inside the outline. The red lines are adjacent to the outline. Stitching right inside the outline will result in very good definition of the finished design.

4 Turn your quilt top over. With non-pointed scissors, trim away the batting that is not behind the motif. Clip close to the stitched line, but don't be overly picky. The reason you stitch just inside the outline is to give you extra room for trimming and still keep the batting inside the line of the design. Cut away all batting shown in the green area (page 98). Be careful here—it is easy to cut your quilt top.

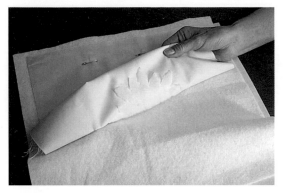

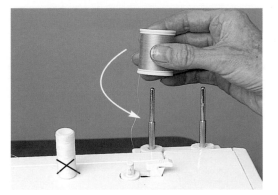

TIPS FOR CUTTING TRAPUNTO BATTING

Having a hard time lifting and cutting the thick batting? The next time you try this technique, add a thin piece of bleached muslin between your quilt top and the trapunto batting at Step 1. It can be easier to lift the batting with the muslin. I use this method more and more, although several students have given me a "thumbs down" on the idea.

5 At this point the quilt top can be made into a sandwich like any other quilt top. Layer it with your cotton batting and backing. Baste the sandwich carefully.

6 Exchange the water-soluble thread in your needle for your quilting thread NOW.

7 Quilt all the lines of the design directly on the design lines. Follow the quilting diagram. You will stitch right next to the water-soluble stitches. It looks a little messy now, but the final result will not have the double line of stitching.

8 Add background stitching in areas surrounding the motif. This will make the motif stand out even more.

9 Complete all your quilting and bind your quilt. Immerse your quilt in clear, tepid water. Let it soak for 1–2 minutes, and swish it around by hand for a few seconds. All the water-soluble thread will dissolve and, if you used a water-rinseable marker, all those marks will disappear as well.

Hand Quilting Using this Trapunto Technique

If you love to hand quilt, you can still add this no-stuff trapunto technique to your bag of quilting tricks.

These tips assume you know how to hand quilt.

Be selective when choosing a quilting motif. Choose designs that do not have a lot of interior lines, otherwise you will have to do a lot of quilting through very thick batting. Look for designs that depend mostly on the outline of the design for their shape. In the few instances where you do have to stitch through the thick batting, you may have to resort to the "stab" method of quilting, rather than being able to load up your needle with stitches.

Few interior lines.   Many interior lines.

Some cotton batting is difficult to hand quilt. If you want to hand quilt with this technique, it will be easier if you use polyester batting for both the trapunto and the overall battings.

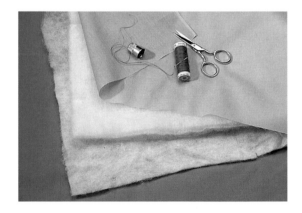

Even though you don't care to free-motion machine quilt, use your machine to free-motion baste the trapunto batting with water-soluble thread. (Read Steps 1-5, Machine Trapunto, pages 18-19.) Don't worry about what the machine stitches look like. Who cares if they are jagged and uneven? Machine quilting isn't your interest, and these machine stitches will be gone when the quilt is finished. After you have trimmed away all the batting from areas you don't want to trapunto, layer your quilt and baste with your favorite basting method. Then hand quilt.

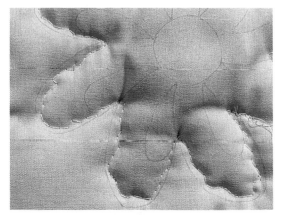

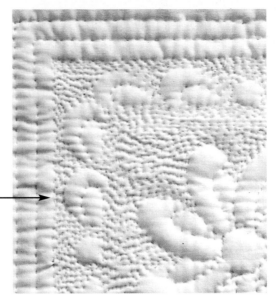

Back of Quilt

After your quilt is completed and immersed in water (Step 8 in the machine trapunto method, page 19) the only stitches that will remain will be your hand stitches. There will be no machine stitches left in your quilt, and there will be no cuts or holes in the backing.

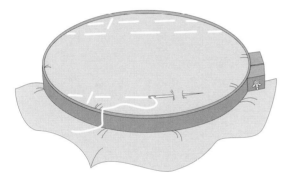

Most hand quilters thread baste. If you do, you might want to try the basting method on page 23.

Good hand quilting designs.

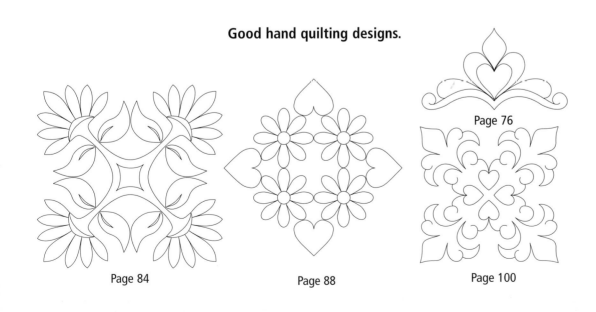

Page 76

Page 84

Page 88

Page 100

Basting for Beauty

A good job of basting your quilt sandwich makes quilting much easier. This isn't the most exciting part of making a quilt, but it is very important. Call on your Quilt Spirit (page 43) if you procrastinate at this step.

Consider. . .

With the machine trapunto technique explained in this book, the trapunto batting is added before basting. The following photographs demonstrate how the added stress of the trapunto batting can warp your quilt top, and why good basting is so important.

TRAPUNTO WARP
After you have added the trapunto batting to your quilt top, you may notice some wavy areas. This is normal. The trapunto batting has stretched the fabric slightly.

BACKGROUND STRESS
Depending on the thickness of the batting, dense background stitching can also warp your quilt.

ONE CANCELS THE OTHER
Fortunately, if you stitch dense background quilting next to an area with trapunto batting, each technique cancels out the waviness created by the other.

QUILT BACKING
Make sure your quilt backing lies flat. This is especially true of a pieced backing. I use a lot of spray sizing or starch and iron carefully before making the quilt sandwich.

WRINKLED BATTING
Batting is often packaged tightly, causing wrinkles. If you tumble the batting in a warm dryer for a few minutes, the heat will relax the wrinkles.

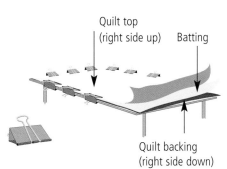

Quilt top (right side up)   Batting

Quilt backing (right side down)

WHERE TO BASTE
Layer your quilt sandwich on a large flat surface. Large tables and hard floors are great. Smooth each layer as you lay it in place. Large black office clips are very handy for holding the edges of your quilt sandwich to a table.

Three Basting Methods

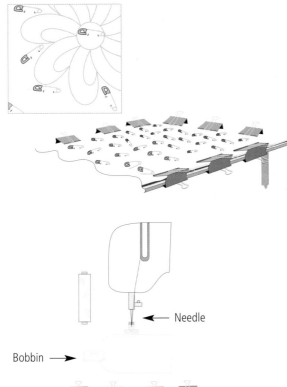

PIN BASTING

Machine quilters often pin baste their quilts with safety pins. Begin pinning in the center and gently smooth the layers as you go. Check to make sure the back of your quilt sandwich is free of puckers.

Put extra pins right next to areas where you have added trapunto batting. The thick batting slightly lifts the quilt top off the overall batting and if you pin securely it prevents shifting and slipping during quilting.

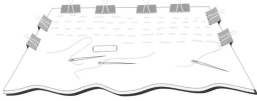

Needle

Bobbin

THREAD BASTING

What? Thread basting for machine quilting? Yes, if you use water-soluble basting thread. You don't have to worry about stitching over the basting because this thread will dissolve when you immerse your quilt in water.

Thread baste by hand or with a long basting stitch on your sewing machine. You must put water-soluble thread in both the needle and in the bobbin. If you thread baste a large quilt in your machine, you will need to pin baste it first. After it is thread basted, you remove the pins.

I find that thread basting large quilts by hand is just as fast as pinning and then basting them on the machine.

One benefit of thread basting is that you eliminate the weight of all those safety pins and you no longer have to stop and remove pins while you quilt.

SPRAY BASTING

There are many fabric adhesive sprays available that are handy for basting. Spray one layer at a time and carefully smooth it to the adjoining surface. Carefully read and follow the directions on the product you buy.

I use these sprays on smaller quilts only, because the glue loses its effectiveness after a few days.

Most of these spray glues warn against breathing the vapors. Listen to the warnings.

Please use these sprays outside or in an area where there is excellent ventilation.

Little Things Mean A Lot

The best quilting skills in the world only enhance the visual effect of your quilt if they can be seen.

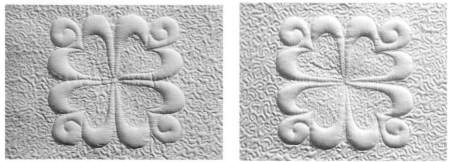

Broadcloth or Muslin   Cotton Sateen

FABRIC

The way light hits your fabric is critical to the visual impact your quilt makes. Rich colors can dramatize your piecing, but quilting stitches are seen best on medium to light value solid-colored fabrics. Cotton sateen has a sheen that catches and reflects light and adds depth and richness to your stitching. It also photographs beautifully for those of you who are interested in entering juried contests where good slides are important.

   The same thread and fabric color were used in both samples shown above; only the type of fabric is different.

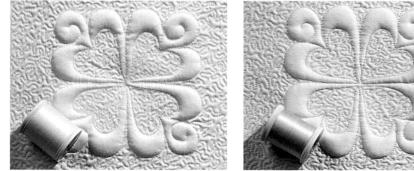

Matching Thread   Slightly Darker Thread

THREAD

If you stitch with thread that is a little darker than your fabric, you will add more depth to the overall look. Quilting stitches always make indentations in the surface and create shadows where the stitches are. Thread that is a bit darker than the fabric enhances these shadows and the illusion of depth is greater. It is true that using thread the exact color of your fabric will disguise your mistakes, but you are a better quilter than you give yourself credit for. You don't need to hide those few little character marks.

   The fabric in the samples above is the same; only the thread color is different.

One great benefit of stitching with a slightly darker thread is that it is much easier to see while you are stitching.

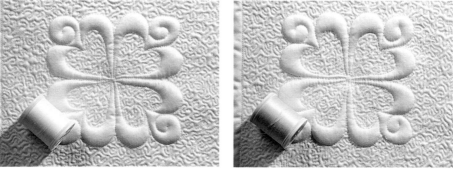

White Thread   Light Gray Thread

The above theory is also true when stitching on white fabric. Both samples shown above were stitched on a white cotton sateen; the only difference is the thread color.

Canterbury Tales, 83'' x 83''
Hari Walner

The border of this quilt is an example of using a quilting design as an appliqué pattern, as suggested in Idea Four (page 36). The edge of the quilting design was appliquéd to the printed fabric so the quilting design became part of the pieced top.* The dark, solid sateen fabric was hand-dyed to be compatible with the print. After the top was pieced and appliquéd, the trapunto batting was added. The quilting was done with threads slightly darker than the fabrics. I think the quilt would have been a bit prettier if I would have also added trapunto batting to the back of the designs in the diamonds and triangles. Next time.

*A sincere thank you to appliqué teacher/artist Alice Wilhoit of Anna, Texas for her last minute help in appliquéing most of this border. The smoothly turned edges are hers.

Paris, 59'' x 59''
Linda Taylor

Linda's artistry with a long-arm commercial quilting machine is truly evident in this quilt. Her graceful echo quilting is almost magical in the way it reinforces and accents the quilting motif. Because of her facility with this machine, she was able to quickly add the trapunto batting. She used the cording effect in all the diamonds in the border to accent her simple free-motion extemporaneous quilting. The quilting design is Paris (page 100) turned on point in the block and then one-quarter of the Paris design was quilted in each corner of the block.

Here are ideas you may want to explore and combine with the basic free-motion machine quilting and trapunto techniques.

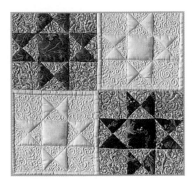

IDEA ONE:
Trapunto Block by Block

IDEA TWO:
Cornerstone Quilting

IDEA THREE:
Sew AcCORDINGly

IDEA FOUR:
Appliqué and Trapunto

IDEA FIVE:
It's Okay to Fake Appliqué

IDEA SIX:
Tiny Trapunto

IDEA SEVEN:
Personal Expressions

Trapunto Block by Block

See Shirley's quilt on page 62.

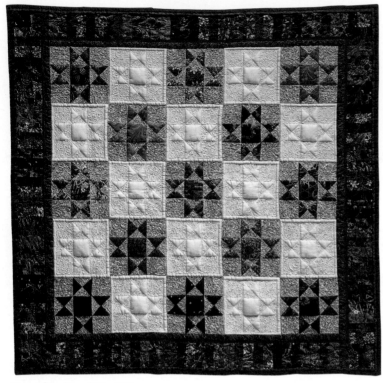

Star After Star, 36'' x 36''
Hari Walner

We often spend a lot of time wringing our hands, trying to decide which quilting pattern will look best when stitched into our quilt. Sometimes a simple solution is all that is called for. When making a pieced, two-block quilt with an alternate plain block, consider using the piecing design as your quilting design in the alternate block. The quilting pattern will reinforce the piecing pattern, giving your quilt a finished, well-thought-out look.

Look for a block with pieces that are not too large. If you trapunto a very large plain patch, it can look like a pillow. Consider using blocks that have a definite light-dark pattern to help you decide which areas you want to stuff and which areas you want to render in a background stitch.

You will need:
- Basic trapunto supplies (page 17)
- Two-block quilt, alternating plain blocks with pieced blocks

This example uses a traditional nine-patch block, the Ohio Star.

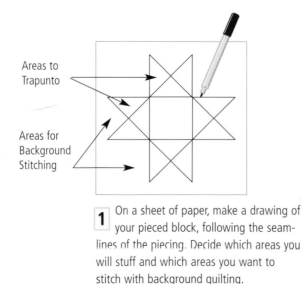

Areas to Trapunto

Areas for Background Stitching

1 On a sheet of paper, make a drawing of your pieced block, following the seamlines of the piecing. Decide which areas you will stuff and which areas you want to stitch with background quilting.

2 With your marking tool, mark all the lines of the piecing/quilting pattern in all the plain blocks on the quilt top.

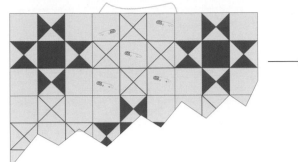 

3 Cut a piece of trapunto batting large enough to cover a block design. Pin it to the back of a plain block.

This is what the back of your quilt top will look like.

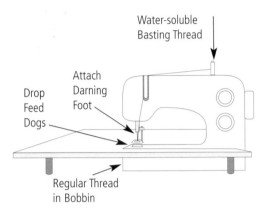

Water-soluble Basting Thread

Attach Darning Foot

Drop Feed Dogs

Regular Thread in Bobbin

4 Thread your needle with water-soluble basting thread. Put white, or a light-colored neutral, regular thread in your bobbin. Attach a darning foot or free-motion quilting foot to your machine. Drop or cover the feed dogs.

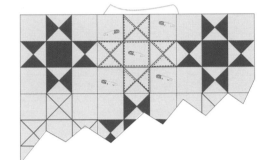

5 Free-motion stitch just inside the lines, on the side where the "puffiness" will be. In this illustration, the water-soluble stitching is shown in red. Using a free-motion stitching technique for this step will prevent you from needing to constantly turn your quilt. Don't worry if your stitching lines are not perfectly straight. The water-soluble thread will be dissolved later.

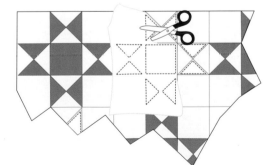

6 Turn your quilt top over and trim the thick batting away from the areas you don't want to trapunto. Repeat this procedure on all of the blocks you are going to trapunto, including the pieced blocks if you intend to trapunto them.

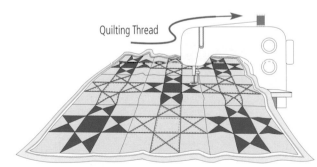

Quilting Thread

7 Layer your quilt sandwich. With your quilting thread back in the needle, quilt on the marked lines in the plain blocks and in the seamlines of the pieced blocks. Add background stitching to enhance the trapunto areas. Bind. Finish by immersing in water as demonstrated in Machine Trapunto page 19, Step 9.

Cornerstone Quilting

Cabin in the Woods,
14" x 16"
Cheryl Phillips

The letters were quilted with long narrow scallops to imitate chiseled wood.

Cornerstone Quilting is the reverse of machine trapunto. It is especially useful for lettering. It almost looks engraved. Simple poems and dates are possible uses. You can also "engrave" a simple quilting design.

For this technique the trapunto batting does not need to be thick. One layer of a cotton batting works well. You can trim it very close for good definition and it doesn't create too much bulk in the areas surrounding the indented design.

It is not necessary to use water-soluble thread to baste the first batting. You will have a double line of stitching on the outline of the letters, but this only reinforces the carved look. Try it both ways and see which one you like better. Use a machine quilting thread that is darker than the fabric to increase the illusion of depth (see page 24).

The following example shows only the lettering, but you should always assemble your entire quilt top before adding the trapunto batting.

The alphabet on pages 92-93 was used in this example. The letters were enlarged to 125% of the size they appear, then marked and stitched.

You will need:

• Basic trapunto supplies (page 17)

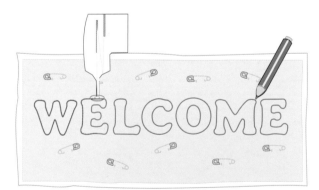

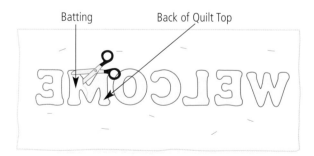

1 Mark your design on the front of the quilt top. Pin a piece of batting to the back of your quilt top in the areas you want to recede. Do not use a backing for this step. You can use water-soluble thread for this step, but it is not necessary. Free-motion stitch around each letter. Remember to stitch the insides of letters that have a center shape (the O in this example).

2 Turn your quilt top over and trim the batting away from the inside of the letters, leaving the batting on the inside of the O. Trim the batting as close to the edge of the letters as you can.

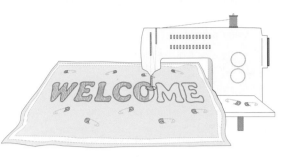

3 When the thick batting is trimmed away from all the areas you want to recede, layer the entire quilt top with a cotton batting and backing. Until you add this final batting, there is no batting behind the letters. Baste securely to avoid shifting and slipping while you quilt.

4 Stitch back over the previous outline stitches on each letter. This double stitching adds definition to the letters. In the drawing, the letters were stitched with simple free-motion vertical straight lines very close together.

Lettering and Spacing

The easiest part of using letters and numbers in your quilt art is the tracing and stitching. What helps make lettering beautiful is the spacing between the letters. Graceful lettering does not mean precise, equal measurement between letters. An easy way to place letters is to consider how much space each letter is surrounded by. The space around a letter affects the letters on each side of it.

A L C T Y ← These letters vary in the amount of space before, after, and within the letter.

M N H I U ← In contrast, M, N, H and I have almost no space on either side of them.

QUILT

QUILT

We take this variation in spacing into consideration when placing one letter next to another. This means some letters will actually be closer together, sometimes even overlap, in order to look right. In the printing industry, this space-adjusting is call kerning. Here is an example:

The spacing in the above word QUILT is precisely the same between each letter. Notice how the L and T seem farther apart than the others. This is because L and T are surrounded with more space. The U, I and L also seem a bit close to each other because there is very little space surrounding the U and I and the left side of L.

Here the L and T have been moved closer together and the U, I, and L have been separated just slightly. The word QUILT now looks more balanced.

Two Thoughts

1 If you are going to trapunto the letters, leave enough space between them so you can background quilt around the letters. This spacing between the letters is not as crucial if you are using the cornerstone technique.

2 Kerning is a matter of taste. Perfection is an impossible goal. Just do your best and get on with your quilting.

IDEA THREE
Sew AcCORDINGly

See Jerry's quilt on page 50, Margie's quilt on page 55, and Barbara's quilt on page 57.

Love Knot, 20'' x 20''
Hari Walner
Quilted by Sue Danielson

Here are three easy ways to achieve a corded, or Celtic, effect with machine trapunto. Depending on your overall quilt design and other quilting/trapunto techniques you may be using, you need to decide which technique or combination of techniques works best for you.

Cording Technique #1

(free-motion, feed dogs down)

A section of Knot Crazy (page 80) was used for this example. Cording Technique #1 is useful when the design you want to cord has curves and points.

You will need:
• Basic trapunto supplies (page 17)

1 Mark all black lines of the design onto your quilt top.

2 Pin very thick batting or several layers of thinner batting to the back of the quilt top. Do not use backing. With water-soluble thread in the needle of your machine and regular thread in the bobbin, free-motion stitch down the middle of the two lines, where you see the red dashed line in the drawing.

Back of Quilt Top

3 Turn the quilt top over and trim, leaving a generous margin of batting on each side of the stitched line. With this design, about 1/8'' was left on each side of the line of stitching.

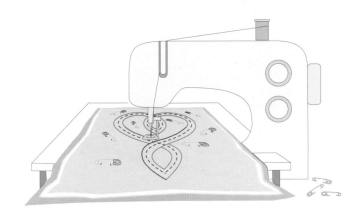

4 After all excess batting is trimmed away, layer your quilt sandwich. Baste well.

5 With regular thread back in the needle, free-motion quilt on all the black lines of the design. When you are quilting, this looks a little rough with the stitching down the middle of the "cording." Don't worry. As soon as the quilt is immersed in water, the water-soluble thread will disappear and you will have the corded effect.

Cording Techniques #2 and #3
(double needle, feed dogs up)

You will need to use a double needle in your sewing machine for the first part of these two techniques. Most machines (provided they at least have a zigzag capability) can handle a 6mm-wide double needle. Some of the newer machines can use a wider double needle. Be sure the throat plate on your machine is the one you use for zigzag and decorative stitches. The throat plate with the small, round hole will not accommodate a double needle, and its use will result in broken needles.

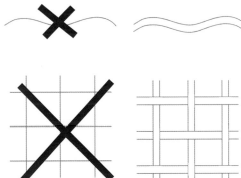

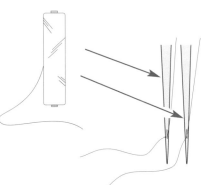

1 Mark the entire design on your quilt top. Mark both sides of the cording because the actual quilting will be done with a single needle, and you will find that having both lines marked eliminates confusion.

2 Thread both eyes of your double needle with water-soluble basting thread. Regular white thread or water-soluble thread will work for bobbin thread. Loosen your top tension.*

*A loose top tension allows the top thread to completely bury itself in the fabric and lets the bobbin thread swing comfortably from needle to needle on the underside. All machines are different. Experiment.

Cording Technique #2

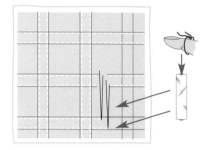 

1 Pin a piece of thick batting to the back of your quilt top. Using a double needle and a long stitch length, stitch on the lines you want to look corded. You may need to stitch at a slower speed. Don't worry if the width of your double needle does not exactly match the width of your drawn lines.

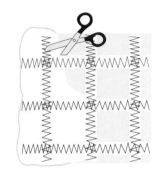

2 Notice the zigzag stitch pattern covering the batting on the back of your quilt. This is caused by your bobbin serving two needles. Leave intact the batting that is under the zigzag stitches and trim away all the rest of the batting. Trim so the batting is a tiny bit narrower than the drawn lines on the front of your quilt top.

3 Layer and baste your quilt sandwich together. For your final quilting, use a single needle and your regular quilting thread. Quilt on all the lines of your design. If your grid has an under/over pattern, you will be grateful that you marked both sides of the cording. When your quilt is completely finished, immerse in water and the water-soluble stitching lines will disappear.

Cording Technique #3

Cheryl Phillips, from Fruita, Colorado, shares this cording technique with us. It works great.

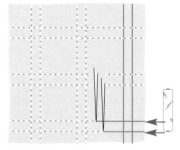 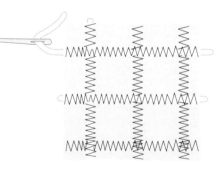

1 Do not pin a thick batting on the back of your quilt top. With the double needle and water-soluble thread, stitch on the lines of your design. Your marked design lines may be wider than your double needle. Just stitch down the center of your marked lines. Keep your upper thread tension very loose.

2 Turn your quilt top over. With a large craft needle and cotton upholstery cording, thread the cording under the zigzag stitching on the back of your quilt top. The thickness of the cording will depend on how wide the channel of your double needle is. The wider the double needle, the thicker the cording. For a common 6mm double needle, 1/8''-1/16'' cording works well.

3 Cut the cording when it crosses over another piece of cording. If you overlap the cording at the intersections, you will have a thick bump.

4 After all cording has been threaded, layer your quilt sandwich. For your final quilting, use a single needle, regular thread, and stitch on each side of the cording. (See Cording Technique #2 above, Step 3.)

COMPARE THESE
CORDING TECHNIQUES

	GOOD	NOT-SO-GOOD
TECHNIQUE #1	• Enables you to stitch corded quilting designs with tight curves without having to turn your quilt in the machine. Very useful for large quilts because it is difficult to turn a large quilt while it is in the machine.	• Not easy to create beautiful, straight grids. • When basting the thick batting, you must eyeball the distance from the basting line when you cut away.
TECHNIQUE #2	• Because you have the assistance of feed dogs, you can create beautiful, straight grid work, as well as gentle curves. • Zigzag pattern gives you a good guide for trimming the thick batting.	• Does not allow stitching tight curves without turning your quilt in the machine. • Feed dogs may drag pieces of the batting into the bobbin case if you do not use an inner backing or water-soluble stabilizer.
TECHNIQUE #3	• Eliminates trimming thick trapunto batting. • Good for achieving straight grids and gentle curves.	• Does not allow stitching tight curves without turning your quilt in the machine. • Cording width is limited by the width of your double needle, which determines how wide the channel to thread the cording will be.

TIP

When using the double needle, Technique #2, your feed dogs are up and touching the batting. If this makes you wary, put a piece of thin unbleached muslin or water-soluble stabilizer underneath the thick batting. Then just trim it away when you trim the excess batting. It will be buried in the quilt sandwich.

IDEA FOUR
Appliqué and Trapunto

This section is not about appliqué techniques (see Bibliography, page 109). It is about adding trapunto to appliqué motifs and appliquéing quilting motifs.

First, we will use the Machine Trapunto technique (pages 17-19) with an appliquéd motif. Following this are two other methods that might interest you. Then, we will explore the possibilities of using a quilting motif for appliqué. These demonstrations use the Sparkling Dahlia design on page 98. It is always best to assemble your entire quilt top before adding the trapunto batting.

You will need:
- Basic machine trapunto supplies (page 17)
- Fabric for appliqué motifs

Machine Trapunto with Appliqué

1 Appliqué the motifs onto your base fabric with your favorite appliqué method. Trim the base fabric away from the back of the motif. Pin a thick trapunto batting behind the motif. Do not use a quilt backing now.

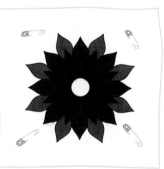

2 With water-soluble basting thread in the needle, baste the trapunto batting to the underside of your appliqué motif. Stitch around the perimeter of the entire motif, staying 1/16'' – 1/8'' inside the edge.

Water-soluble Thread

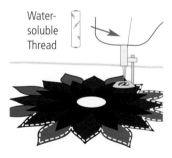

3 Turn your quilt top over and trim away all the batting, except that which is behind the appliqué motif. Trim as close as you can to the line of basting stitches.

Back of Quilt Top

4 When all the excess trapunto batting has been trimmed away, layer and baste your quilt sandwich. Use regular quilting thread and quilt right next to each seamline, staying on the side of the line that the appliqué was basted onto. You may choose to change thread colors often. Some quilters use monofilament nylon thread in these situations because of its transparency.

When the quilting is finished and you have put the binding on your quilt, immerse it in water as explained in Step 9, Machine Trapunto, page 19.

Quilting Thread Now in Needle

Don't forget this time-honored method.

1 Appliqué the motifs onto your base fabric with your favorite appliqué method.

Back of Quilt Top →

2 Do not trim away the fabric behind the motifs. Cut small slits and insert tiny pieces of batting into each element of the design. You will not need to sew the slits closed because they will immediately be sandwiched, basted, and quilted.

3 Layer your quilt sandwich and baste well. The basted quilt top, overall batting, and backing will hold the stuffed areas in place until it is quilted. Quilt around each design element to define it and to insure that the trapunto stuffing doesn't move.

Next, thanks to new products. . .

Appliqué as in #1 above. Cut the base fabric away from behind the motif.

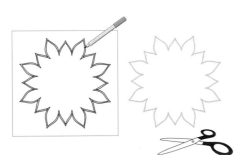

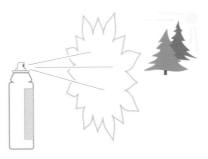

Back of Quilt Top

1 Trace the outline of your motif on a sheet of paper. Make a second smaller outline about 1/8'' inside the original drawing. Cut a piece of batting in the shape and size of the smaller outline. Thick cotton battings seem to hold their shape better for this technique.

2 With one of the new temporary spray adhesives, spray individual pieces of shaped batting. Be sure to spray the side that will fit on the back of the appliqué motif. Follow the instructions on the product you buy. Spray outside to avoid breathing the vapors.

NOTE: If you want two or three layers of cotton batting for more loft, cut squares of the batting, spray lightly, and adhere them together before you cut out your motif.

3 With the sticky side facing the back of the quilt top, accurately place the shaped batting onto the back of the appliqué motif that is to be stuffed. When all motifs have been backed with the extra batting, layer your quilt sandwich, baste well, and quilt.

Quilting Pattern Appliqué

1 Trace the entire quilting design onto a piece of plain, light-colored fabric. Trim around the outer perimeter of the design and leave a turn-under allowance for your favorite appliqué technique. Many quilters prefer to cut the turn-under allowance as they appliqué, making the motif easier to handle.

2 Stitch the appliqué design onto a base fabric by hand or machine. The outer points of this design are quite sharp. You may prefer to round them off a little bit.

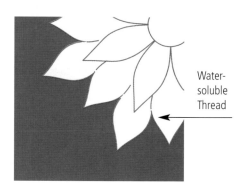

Water-soluble Thread

3 Once the motifs have been sewn and the quilt top is complete, trapunto the motifs. For this demonstration, we will use the Machine Trapunto method (see pages 17-19). With water-soluble thread, stitch $1/16''$-$1/8''$ inside the outer perimeter. Trim the excess batting away, leaving batting only behind the motif. Make your quilt sandwich and baste securely.

INTERIOR LINES. Use a thread that is slightly darker than the fabric you used for your appliqué motif.

EXTERIOR QUILTING LINES. Stitch all the way around the appliqué, right next to the edge, on the base fabric. Use a thread that is slightly darker than the base fabric. This will help accent the motif. Use the same thread for any background quilting you might do.

4 Quilt the appliqué and the rest of the quilt. Bind the quilt. If you have used the Machine Trapunto method, immerse in water as explained in Step 9, page 19.

It's Okay to Fake Appliqué

See Loraine's quilt on page 66 and Josie's quilt on page 54.

This technique is included in this book because the image is created without the bulk of seam allowances, making it very easy to trapunto.

The Fake Appliqué method is actually a controlled painting/stenciling technique. It allows us to have beautiful appliqué shapes and colors on our quilts without the tedium of stitching each shape. Several designs in this book can be adapted for use with this freezer paper painting.

The design used in the demonstration is Simplicity, page 81.

You will need:

- Solid, light-colored fabric
- Freezer paper larger than your design
- Craft knife to cut the freezer paper
- Device to mist the paint
- Fabric paint or dye
- Breathing mask and eye protectors

Simplicity, 24'' x 24''
Hari Walner

In this little quilt, the design is used in one size for the misting and a reduced version of the same design for the quilting. The trapunto technique was applied to the fake appliqué and the plain quilting pattern.

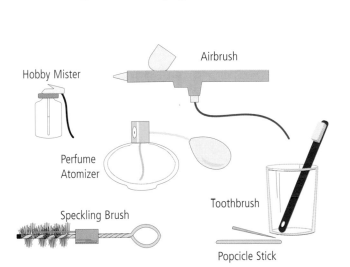

Hobby Mister

Airbrush

Perfume Atomizer

Speckling Brush

Toothbrush

Popcicle Stick

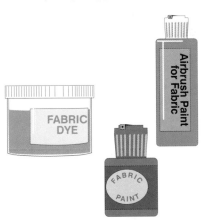

FABRIC DYE

Airbrush Paint for Fabric

FABRIC PAINT

Many tools can be used to mist an image. . . a perfume atomizer, an airbrush, or a hobby mister driven by canned air. If you want a smooth, well-defined image, avoid using a tool that makes a coarse spray.

If you would like a spotty, random image, use a speckling brush. You can also spatter the paint with an old toothbrush. Just touch the tip of the bristles into paint poured on a plate and drag a nail or popcicle stick back toward you over the tips of the brush.

'There are a variety of name-brand fabric paints and dyes that will work just fine. Read each label carefully for application and setting instructions. Many art supply stores carry several brands.

For the sharpest image, use this misting technique on your fabric before you assemble your quilt top. If you mist on pieced fabric, be sure the seams are ironed open and are as flat as possible.

Cutting Surface

1 Place a large piece of freezer paper on top of your design, shiny side down. Trace the design using a pencil or permanent marker. Do not use a water-based marker since ink residue may run onto your fabric later.

2 With a craft knife, cut out the areas you want to mist with paint. In this demonstration, the petals and center of the flower are cut out. Use a good cutting surface and cut accurately. The cutting mat you use with your rotary cutter works fine.

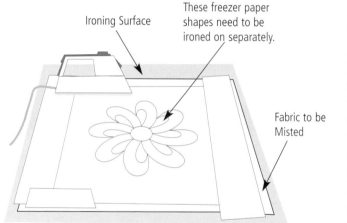

Ironing Surface

These freezer paper shapes need to be ironed on separately.

Fabric to be Misted

3 Iron the freezer paper onto your fabric, shiny side down. Make sure all edges of the design adhere to the fabric. When ironing the design shown, the flower center and each paper shape between the petals must also be ironed on. The fabric should show through the cut-out design. This works best if it is a single layer of fabric, although you can mist fabric that has been pieced. At this stage the quilt sandwich has not been put together. Make sure all the areas you want to stay the original color are covered with freezer paper. If they are not, you can iron additional pieces of freezer paper onto these areas. You do not want the color to touch these areas.

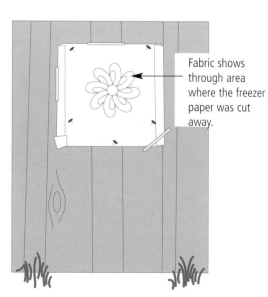

Fabric shows through area where the freezer paper was cut away.

4 Tape or tack the fabric with the freezer paper to a vertical surface outside. Protect any surfaces you don't want misted. Be very careful not to let the freezer paper pull away from the fabric.

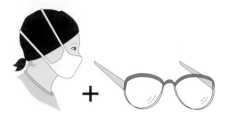

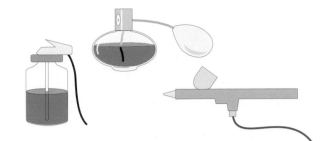

5 Put on your breathing mask. Even though you are outside, you should at least use a painter's mask. If you don't wear eyeglasses, consider using goggles. Always follow directions and suggestions that the manufacturer of the paint or dye recommends for safety.

6 Fill your misting/spraying device with fabric paint or dye. Perfume atomizers usually work best with a thin solution. If your tools come with directions, read them. Experiment before you mist meaningful fabric.

TIPS FOR MISTED FAKE APPLIQUÉ

• **The object of this technique is to mist the fabric. If your fabric gets wet the color will bleed under the freezer paper and your image will have ragged edges.**

• **Clean your misting equipment as quickly as possible. The paint will dry and may clog your tool.**

• **If you want to mist an image that is lighter than your fabric, you will need to use a fabric paint that is opaque and lighter than your fabric. A transparent paint or dye will not lighten your fabric, even if the paint color is lighter than your fabric.**

• **When you are misting the fabric it helps to have a small piece of the original fabric in sight, out of range of the mist. This will help you gauge how much your fabric color is changing.**

7 Mist the area where the fabric shows through. Do not saturate the fabric or the paint will creep under the freezer paper and you will lose the sharp definition of your design.

8 When you have misted the fabric so the image is the color you want, peel the freezer paper from your fabric. Since the color was only misted on, it only takes a minute or so to dry. Follow the directions that came with your fabric paint or dye to set the image permanently. After the color is set, use the fabric in your quilt. The appliquéd shape, without the bulk of the appliqué turn-under allowance, makes the image easy to trapunto.

Reverse Fake Appliqué

When you reverse the use of the freezer paper, you reverse the
result you get when you mist the image.

Simply Reversed, 17" x 21"
Hari Walner
Quilted by Sue Danielson

1 When you cut the design out of the
freezer paper, use the pieces of freezer
paper in the shape of the actual design
rather than the background. This will cause
your image to remain the color of the fabric while the surrounding areas receive the
paint or dye.

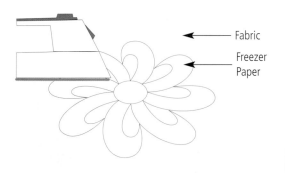

Fabric

Freezer
Paper

2 Iron the freezer paper with the design
image, not the background image. Be
sure to iron the edges down.

3 When you mist the fabric now, you
are misting the background of the
image. You don't necessarily need to completely cover the background. Just
feathering the color around the edges is
sometimes very effective.

4 Peel the freezer paper away. The
image is still the color of the original
fabric. The fabric has been made darker by
the paint color. On some designs you may
need to trace interior design lines before
you quilt.

THE QUILT SPIRIT

I often remind myself of the need for my Quilt Spirit. There are several ways my Quilt Spirit helps me.

In creating our art, there are times when the next step is not one of our favorite things to do. This can be ironing yardage, cutting, basting, or any number of steps in the process that in themselves are not highly creative—the chores that make us wish we had an apprentice. Some days we do not mind these steps, other days they are a real inconvenience. Worse, we often use these chores as an excuse not to finish our projects.

When these chores fall on a day that makes me think I would rather watch paint dry, I let my Quilt Spirit remind me that the step in front of me is the most fun available that day, anywhere. Well, far be it from me to ignore having a good time. I iron, I cut, I baste . . . with vigor. I find I am actually having fun. Why was I dragging my feet? Thank you, dear Quilt Spirit. By the way, I also need to frequently call on my Housekeeping Spirit.

IDEA SIX
Tiny Trapunto

Surprise Package, 16'' x 20''
Hari Walner

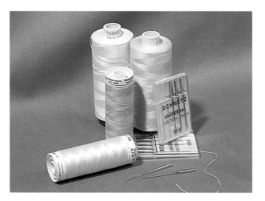

The temptation to make a miniature quilt hits all of us every once in a while and some of us all the time. Idea Six offers pointers that you might find helpful when adding trapunto to your miniature creations.

Although there are no set rules about how small is small, it seems that a real miniature quilt is one in which all the elements: piecing, appliqué, and quilting stitches are scaled down.

Machine quilting is suitable for miniature quilts because the smaller stitches are more in tune with the smaller scale of the rest of the quilt. Here are a few things to consider when adding trapunto to your tiny quilts.

Are we in Kansas yet, Toto? 11'' x 16''
by Cheryl Phillips

NEEDLES AND THREAD

I have found some small size 60 (8) and 65 (9) machine needles that work very well. They leave smaller holes and make it easier to make tight, small quilting designs. I stitch slowly. Since smaller quilts do not go through the trauma that larger quilts do, you can use much lighter-weight thread. Lighter thread means less bulk in the seam allowances as well as making it easier to stitch small designs while free-motion quilting. Machine embroidery thread (60 weight) works very well, as does 80-weight thread.

FABRIC

Choose lightweight fabrics that drape easily if you intend to use your quilt on a tiny bed. If you are going to use your quilt for a wallhanging it is not as important that the fabric drape easily. Although some of the beautiful lightweight fabrics can be expensive, you only need small amounts. Miniature wholecloth quilts can be made with very little fabric.

REGULAR OR OVERALL BATTING

Keep the overall batting very lightweight, especially if you expect to drape your quilt on a doll bed. Thin, low-loft polyester, silk, or cotton batting will work. You can also use cheesecloth (sold in small packets in super-markets); wet it and dry it in the dryer to shrink and fluff it. Two or three layers of cheesecloth make a nice, final batting when you trapunto your tiny quilt. Lightweight flannel is another option.

MAGNIFICATION

My eyes have a birthday every time I do. I use plenty of light and look through a magnifying lamp that swings in front of my sewing machine needle. It magnifies and illuminates.

TRAPUNTO BATTING

When you add a trapunto batting to your tiny quilt, use the same basic trapunto techniques you use for a regular quilt (Machine Trapunto, pages 17-19), except that you cannot use a batting nearly as thick as for a regular quilt. Experiment with different battings to get the effect you want. Sometimes a single layer of cotton batting is all you need.

STITCH LENGTH

When quilting, try to keep stitches short and even. The small needles and lightweight thread make it easier to stitch free-motion curves, but your stitches must be short or the curves will look jagged.

Lavender Blues,
12'' x 12''
Cheryl Phillips

FAKE APPLIQUÉ

The painting/stenciling techniques explained in Idea Five (pages 39-42) allow you to add tiny design elements to your quilt that otherwise would be extremely difficult. The next time you make a tiny quilt, try adding another dimension.

IDEA SEVEN
Personal Expressions

See Julia's quilt on page 63 and Josephine's quilt on page 67.

Quilts are not always made just to cover beds and walls. Quiltmakers make quilts to tell stories, express feelings, send messages, and make statements. We humans love to tell our stories. We quilters often tell them in quilts.

Personal expression quilts are always one-of-a-kind, and therefore, there are never patterns for these quilts. Each one of us can tell our own story, but we cannot tell anyone else's story. We might rely on piecing, appliqué, paint, or a great deal of thread (many kinds) and heavy quilting. We tear, rip, glue, add fancy embellishments, laminated newspaper clippings, and string. We do whatever it takes. Consider adding trapunto to your toolbox for your personal expression quilts.

Even though there cannot be instructions for the quilts shown, the captions give hints as to how the trapunto was used in these quilts.

Stuffed Apples, 48'' x 57''
Hari Walner

This quilt top was pieced in 1987; the second top I had ever pieced. It has been sitting on the shelf ever since because I just didn't know what to do with it. The arbitrary free-form addition of the thick trapunto batting gave it a character I was happy with. A long-arm quilting machine made it easier to attach the very thick trapunto batting—it would have been possible with my sewing machine, just more cumbersome. I dream of some day having one of those handy quilting machines. While quilting, I added birds, leaves, worms, and writing in the border. Maybe because I am now living out of a metropolitan area I was ready to complete my country apple tree.

The Healing Place, 55" x 72"
Cheryl Phillips

This quilt is a wonderful example of trapunto being used in non-traditional ways. Cheryl made this quilt as an expression of particular facets of her life that were coming into focus and ideas that she found inspiring and meaningful. Although Cheryl used areas of trapunto to give physical accents and dimension, it is the cursive freehand writing of tender thoughts and expressions throughout the quilting that adds great emotional and intellectual strength to this quilt.

Loves Me, Loves Me Not, 84'' x 84''
Janet Finley

This lovely Irish Chain quilt is the first quilt Janet has made using this Machine Trapunto technique. Around the edges she used a cording technique explained in Idea Two (pages 33-34). The chain blocks are 7½'' and she machine appliquéd the border. She used three layers of Hobbs Heirloom® cotton for the trapunto batting and one layer for the regular batting. She used 5,470 yards (3 miles) of machine embroidery thread.

Janet kept track of the time spent on each step. Marking, basting, and trimming the trapunto batting, plus quilting the entire quilt; including stippling and stitching the ⅜'' grid around the borders, added up to 277 hours. This does not include piecing, appliqué, or finishing. The quilting pattern is Splendid Susan, found on page 88.

California Snowflake, 85'' x 85''
Lynette Bentley Fulton

Our visions of California are generally not filled with snowflakes, but maybe Lynette's lovely
quilt will change that. Her piecing pattern is Snowflake from Trudie Hughes's book, *On
Point*. Lynette used a cording effect around the outside of the center piecing and used
Extra Loft® by Fairfield for the trapunto batting. Her quilting designs are from the April
family, shown on pages 71-77.

Snowball Magic, 48'' x 48''

Jerry Nichols

Jerry used two simple, but elegant traditional 12'' blocks. Snowball blocks coupled with 54-40 or Fight blocks gave her space to use her excellent free-motion quilting skills. She used Cording Technique #1 suggested in Idea Three (pages 32-33) to outline each of the light fabric areas. This cording effectively accented the small triangles, as well as adding drama to the large areas that contain the quilting design, April Wreath, found on page 74.

Some of Life's Lessons, 43'' x 43''

Leslie Lott

Leslie says she gave this quilt this name because of how much she learned while making it. Piecing with striped fabrics was inspired by Mary Mashuta's book *Stripes in Quilts*. Her choice of soft, earthy colors gives *Some of Life's Lessons* a warm natural look. Leslie used three layers of Hobbs Heirloom for the trapunto batting. The quilting design is Paris, shown on pages 100-101.

Renaissance, 86'' x 86''
Sue Danielson

Sue's magnificent machine quilting shows up especially well because she used cotton sateen for her solid-colored fabrics and quilted with a thread that was slightly darker than her fabric. Feathered star patterns are her particular favorites and she pieced this one with striking fabrics in diagonal rows. The large light-colored solid square is 11'' and the small light square is 5⅝''. The patterned square is 8''. The quilting designs are from the April design family, pages 71-77. Sue used three layers of cotton for the trapunto batting.

The following page shows the back of this extraordinary quilt.

Back of *Renaissance*

Because these machine trapunto techniques do not leave any blemishes in the fabric, whole cloth quilts can be very effective on both sides, as the back of *Renaissance* shows. (The front is on the facing page.) This quilt owes its success to Sue's superb machine quilting skills, as well as to her choice of fabric (cotton sateen) for the backing.

Nefer Again, 28'' x 42''
Josie McKissick

Josie is interested in Egyptian history and this is her painting of the queen Nefertiti. The border of pyramids and the close grid quilting seem just right for the Egyptian theme. Josie realizes that trapunto should be used only where it is appropriate and so she kept the "stuffed" areas to a minimum so they don't detract from the overall design. She used trapunto where it would be effective, in the hieroglyphics at the bottom of the portrait. These hieroglyphics spell out the quilter's name, JOSIE.

Where the Wildflowers Grow, 55'' x 70''
Margie Evans

Margie is always trying new ideas and techniques, and she enjoyed using Idea Three, Cording Technique #1 (pages 32-33) with the Vermont Leaves designs (page 97) on the border of this quilt. Margie also used a straight cording effect in the tablecloth in this rich little still life. She also used parts of the Zenith design (page 82), and Kansas (page 85).

Calming the Waters, 46'' x 46''
Hank Osborn

Quilting whenever possible is Hank's way of relaxing from his sometimes stressful job as an emergency medical technician, thus the quilt's name. He simplified the traditional Storm at Sea piecing pattern and chose the shell quilting patterns on pages 78-79.

Midnight Star, 39'' x 39''
Barbara Totten

Although she has long been an active craftswoman, *Midnight Star* is Barb's very first quilt.
She pieced the quilt top very carefully, but was a little tentative about free-motion quilting.
Instead, she decided to use Cording Technique #3 (pages 33-35) to accent the center star.
It all added up to a terrific first quilt.

Passing Ships, 40'' x 47''
Ramona Hilton

A graceful modification of a traditional Lady of the Lake block resulted in this lovely three-dimensional piecing effect. To further accent the "sails," Mona corded around the edges of the white triangle. The blocks are 8'' x 10'', the small triangles are 2'' and the large white triangles are 8''. The quilting design is the small triangle from the April design family, page 76.

Flower Boxes, 52'' x 52''

Maureen Newman

Maureen's *Flower Boxes* quilt was pieced in the log cabin style, with the large light square (7'') as the beginning square and the logs each 1'' wide. The illusion of depth is achieved with her choice of fabrics and by adding trapunto batting behind the flower and the lightest "log." Maureen also used a quilting thread that was slightly darker than her fabric. Her trapunto batting was two layers of Fairfield's High Loft®. Her love of the outdoors and flowers is reflected in her choice of the quilting pattern, Sparkling Dahlia, shown on page 98.

Just Do It, 29'' x 29''
Cheryl Osborn

The traditional Cut Glass Dish block drafted 24'' is the center for this quilt. Cheryl knew she didn't have a lot of time to quilt this top by hand, but decided to go ahead and "just do it." Life often imitates art and that is what happened for Cheryl. While she was working on *Just Do It*, she found that the quilt was inspiring her to complete many other projects that were waiting to be finished. Even though this is Cheryl's first attempt at hand quilting, she used the Machine Trapunto technique for hand quilters as explained on pages 20-21. The quilting design is Kansas, page 84.

Fancy That, 35'' x 35''
Josie McKissick

Josie was inspired by a quilt pattern designed by Christine M. Frost she saw in *Traditional Quiltworks'* 4th Annual Christmas Special. It is a modified Young Man's Fancy block. The fabric in areas where the design is quilted is a white-on-white print. The quilting design is the large triangle from the April family, page 75. Notice the pleasing combination of fabric and quilting design in this quilt.

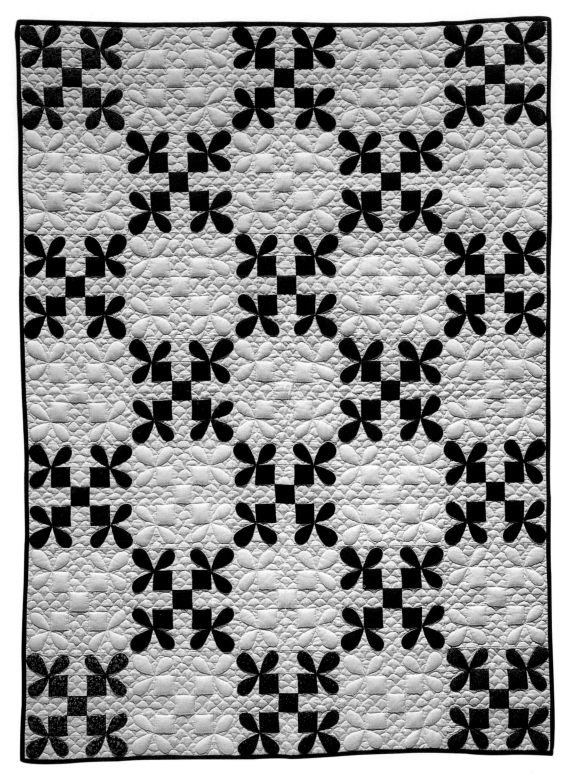

Honey Bee, 40'' x 56''
Shirley Wegert

Long ago, Shirley completed quilts for her children and grandchildren. *Honey Bee* is one of
the many quilts she is now making for great-grandchildren that will someday come along.
The traditional pieced and appliquéd Honey Bee block is 8'' and the plain block is quilted
using the Honey Bee pattern as a quilting design, as suggested In Idea One, pages 28-29.

Autumn Leaves, 50'' x 55''
Julia Payne

Julia is an artist who is inspired by music. When she was looking at the new quilting ideas and designs that are now in this book she kept hearing the familiar song "Autumn Leaves" in her head. She decided that was exactly what she was going to do—make a quilt by painting an autumn tree with fabric and then adding dimension with machine trapunto. She tied lengths of thread to the quilt top to represent the wind, a very novel touch.

Essence of Friendship and Sisterhood, 57'' x 57''

Cynthia Catlin

This quilt is another example of how trapunto can be used in non-traditional ways. Cynthia was commissioned by the Delta Sigma Theta sorority to make this lovely, one-of-a-kind quilt for a very popular member, Millie Cooper-Murphy. Cynthia drew the beautiful feathers freehand and then used trapunto to add dimension. The background/stipple quilting consists of exquisite, tiny swirls. The names of the sorority sisters are written in the border and the label on the back reads as follows:

Quilt Label

Essence of Friendship and Sisterhood

"The supportive Soror's of Delta Sigma Theta Sorority that know and love Millie, decided to commemorate her 40th birthday by contributing to the development of the artistic expression of eternal friendship and devotion. If Millie's blessings were measured by true friendships and how she touches others' lives, then this wallhanging is just one gauge of how Millie's cup is overflowing. So Millie, when you view this piece, always think of those who wish you much success and eternal friendship."

Country Woman, 32" x 32"
Lessie Osborn

Country Woman is all hand quilted, using the Machine Trapunto technique as explained
on pages 20-21. Using this technique, only hand stitches remain when the quilt is finished.
Lessie has been quilting for most of her life and says she cannot begin to remember
how many quilts she has hand quilted. The piecing pattern is a combination of several
modified traditional block patterns, and the quilting design is Splendid Susan, shown on
pages 88-89.

Anchors Away, 42'' x 42''
Loraine Kendrick-Gray

When Loraine wanted to make something special for her son who is in the Navy, she decided to make him a quilt containing images that would represent his career. His profile was made using the Fake Appliqué technique (Idea Five pages 39-41) and because he has sea duty, Loraine surrounded him with waves and Mariner's Compasses. Trapunto batting was added behind the portrait, the waves, and in the stars. The grid quilting behind the portrait and the straight-line quilting behind the anchors are very complimentary to the piecing.

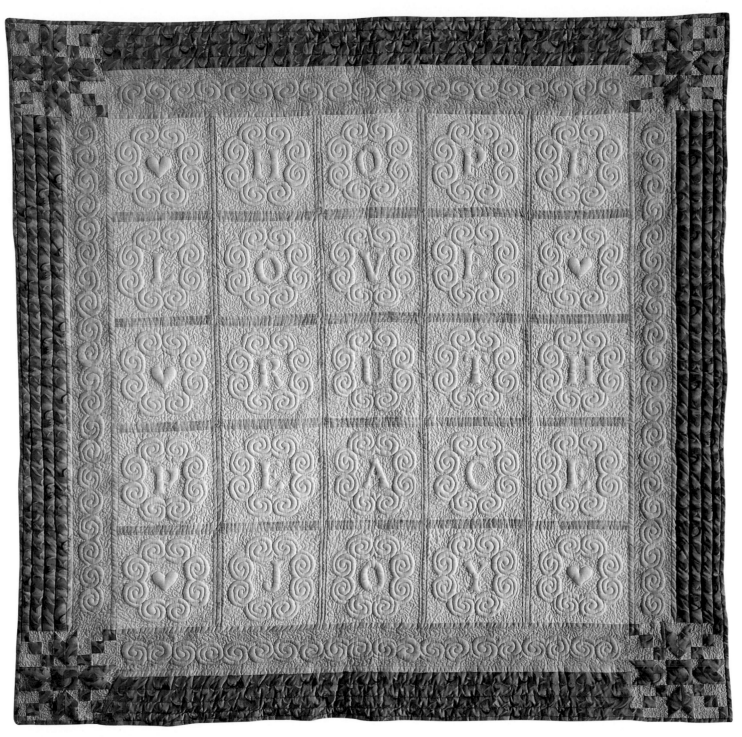

Family Ties, 55'' x 55''
Josephine Thogode

Jo made this quilt for her niece Ruth who had suffered a tragic illness. The quilt was hung on the wall so Ruth could see it from her bed and would be reminded of how much she meant to everyone. Jo used thick polyester for the trapunto batting behind High Tide (pages 90-91) and the letters, and also added cording around the edges of the light blue border. The letters are from the alphabet on page 92.

Half Past Autumn, 84'' x 84''
Sherri Bain Driver

This piecing pattern is the traditional Aunt Sukey's Choice manipulated by Sherri on
her computer. To avoid excess seam lines she appliquéd the small colorful blocks to the
larger plain fabric blocks. The richness of this quilt is a combination of her deliberate
selection of fabrics meshed with an appropriate quilting design. Before quilting, Sherri
basted the entire quilt with water-soluble basting thread on her machine. The quilt
title is derived from the fact that Sherri intended to finish this quilt in the autumn, but
didn't finish it until the following spring, half past autumn. Sherri used the Entwined
designs on pages 94-95 and she modified the large block design for the border quilting.

BE TRUE TO YOURSELF

Sometimes when we are making a quilt, those around us feel a need to offer unsolicited opinions about what we are doing. Although these suggestions may be technically helpful, often they are contrary to our vision for our quilt. Listen to the ideas. If there is a suggestion you can enthusiastically use, wonderful. Thank them and use it. But no matter how persuasive they try to be with their ideas on color, sashing, borders, quilting designs, etc., do not carry through with their ideas simply to avoid hurting their feelings. Implementing ideas that are not in line with your inner goals will only dilute your art. It will be neither your vision nor theirs.

Good art is not done by consensus. Many times these suggestions come from people who are not willing to commit the time and energy to create their own art, so they attempt to be creative through someone else's efforts. Offer to teach your friend, sister, husband, wife, etc., how to make a quilt so they too can enjoy the satisfaction of carrying through with a creative idea. When you need a little extra artistic and moral support in rejecting others' suggestions, call on your Quilt Spirit. She will remind you that your intuition, your vision, and your ideas are just fine, because they really are. You are unique in this whole world—nobody can make your quilts better than you.

THE DESIGNS

All of the qulting designs in this section can be used for the basic machine trapunto technique. Some designs have suggestions for techniques that can be used in addition to the trapunto technique.

There are several families of designs. These designs work well together in projects where you need several compatible shapes. The designs within the families all have the same name, but with different shape designations.

● The heavy black line is the actual design outline.

● The red line adjacent to the outer perimeter of the design is printed to show you where the outline of the design is. It is there only for your reference.

● When you want to baste the trapunto batting onto your quilt top with water-soluble thread, follow the diagram that shows the outline only on a green background.

   If you are making a stencil, this outline on a green background is also a guide to show you what your freezer paper stencil could look like, depending on what elements you decided to render in fake appliqué or whether or not you are doing fake appliqué or reverse fake appliqué.

Try many techniques with one design. Maybe cut the designs in half for triangles and semi-circles. Give your creativity a holiday in a place where there are no judges. Most important, have a good time.

● As explained in the Machine Trapunto section (page 18), when stitching with water-soluble thread, do not stitch directly on the outline, but just inside the outline.

   This will give you a small cutting allowance that will enable you to cut the thick batting just past the line that you will finally quilt. This gives a much sharper edge to your raised motif. For more details, read the Machine Trapunto section, pages 17-19.

● The directional quilting diagram will show you how to quilt the design in as few lines as possible, most often in one continuous line. If present, a ● means to begin stitching. A ■ means the end of the line.

See Lynette's quilt on page 49 and Sue's quilt on pages 52 and 53.

Four of these 7'' motifs make a beautiful, large block design. (See next page.)

7'' Motif

1 Follow the arrows in the shaded diagram when basting the trapunto batting with water-soluble thread. Trim excess batting away from areas shown in green. This drawing also shows how a freezer paper stencil for fake appliqué (pages 39-43) would look.

2 For your final quilting, follow the arrows in these three diagrams. Begin stitching at the ●.

These double lines indicate areas where you will need to backtrack over previous stitches.

Line 1

Line 2

Line 3

April

Half of a 10'' Block

Place dashed line on fold of paper for tracing.

This block design is four motifs (page 71), each positioned 90° from the previous one. Two of the motifs are printed together to make it easy to trace an entire block.

The block takes on a very different character if you turn the individual motifs around and point them in the opposite direction.

1 Trace the design onto a sheet of tracing paper.

2 Follow the arrows when stitching trapunto batting with water-soluble thread. Trim excess batting away from areas shown in green. This diagram also shows what a stencil for fake appliqué (pages 39-43) would look like.

3 See the quilting diagram on the previous page when stitching the design. This block is quilted one-quarter of a section at a time.

See Sue's quilt on pages 52 and 53.

1 Follow the arrows when stitching the trapunto batting with water-soluble thread onto the underside of your quilt top. Trim excess batting away from areas shown in green. The areas shown in white would be the freezer paper stencil for reverse fake appliqué (page 42).

5'' Block

Optional Suggestions For Trapunto Batting

If you want to cut down on your batting trimming time, you can leave the side-center areas of the design "puffed." Whatever you choose, you still need to follow the entire directional quilting diagrams.

Line 1

Line 2

Backtrack

2 Follow the arrows in these diagrams carefully for the most efficient way to quilt this design. Begin stitching at the ● and finish at the ■ . Note that there are some lines where you need to backtrack a little. Don't forget to stitch each side of the design with Line 2.

April

See Hari's quilt on page 25 and Jerry's quilt on page 50.

1 Trace half of the wreath in each half of a sheet of tracing paper.

2 When basting trapunto batting onto the back of quilt top, follow these arrows. Trim excess batting away from areas shown in green.

3 Follow the arrows when doing your final quilting. Begin stitching at the ●. You will stitch the entire line of "swirls" before you stitch the feathers on the outer edge.

Half of a 10½" Wreath

Place dashed line on fold of paper for tracing.

Line 1

1 Follow the arrows when basting the thick trapunto batting. Trim excess batting away from areas shown in green

Finish Line 3   Line 3 begins here

Finish Line 2   Line 2 begins here

2 The two diagrams above show how to stitch the final design. Begin at the ● and finish at the ■ for each line.

Large Triangle

The design above came about by turning the large triangle 180° (not reversing it) and putting the long sides together.

The design on the right results if you turn each of four large April triangles 90° from the previous one and make the points meet in the center.

April

Small Triangle

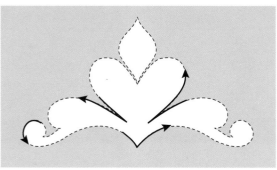

1 Follow the arrows when stitching the trapunto batting onto the back of your quilt. Trim away excess batting from areas shown in green.

2 Carefully follow the arrows for your final quilting. Begin at the ● and finish at the ■. There are a few short lines where you will need to backtrack over previous stitches.

If you use four of these small triangles, each turned 90° from the previous one, you will have another graceful block design.

Two of these triangles will fill a 5'' square with a diagonal design.

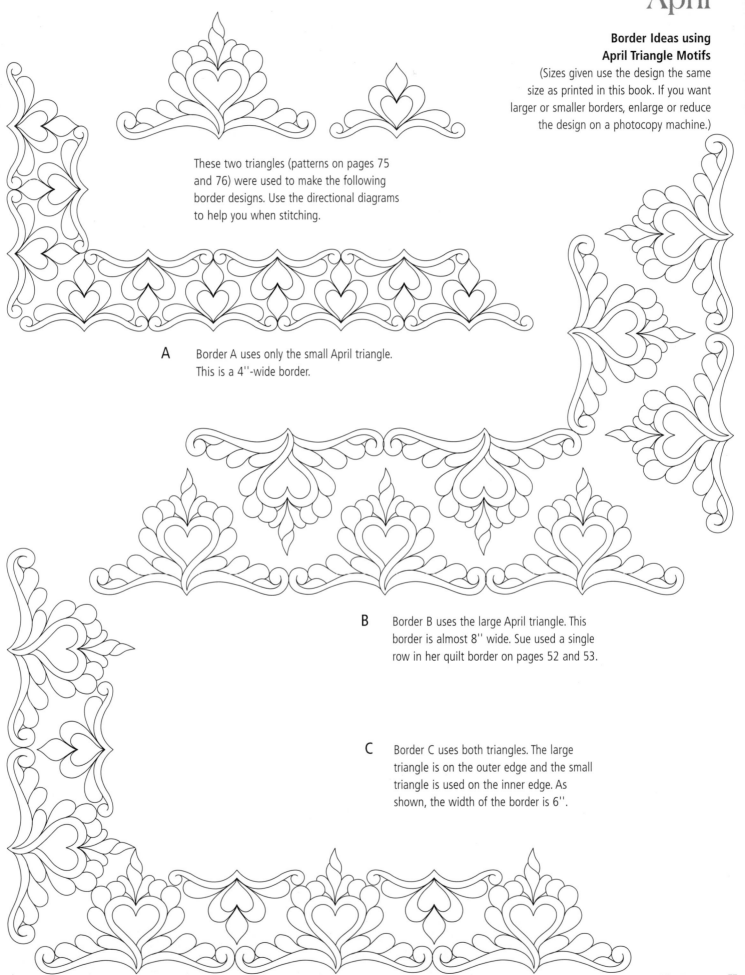

Border Ideas using April Triangle Motifs
(Sizes given use the design the same size as printed in this book. If you want larger or smaller borders, enlarge or reduce the design on a photocopy machine.)

These two triangles (patterns on pages 75 and 76) were used to make the following border designs. Use the directional diagrams to help you when stitching.

A   Border A uses only the small April triangle. This is a 4''-wide border.

B   Border B uses the large April triangle. This border is almost 8'' wide. Sue used a single row in her quilt border on pages 52 and 53.

C   Border C uses both triangles. The large triangle is on the outer edge and the small triangle is used on the inner edge. As shown, the width of the border is 6''.

Shell We Quilt?

See Hank's quilt on page 56.

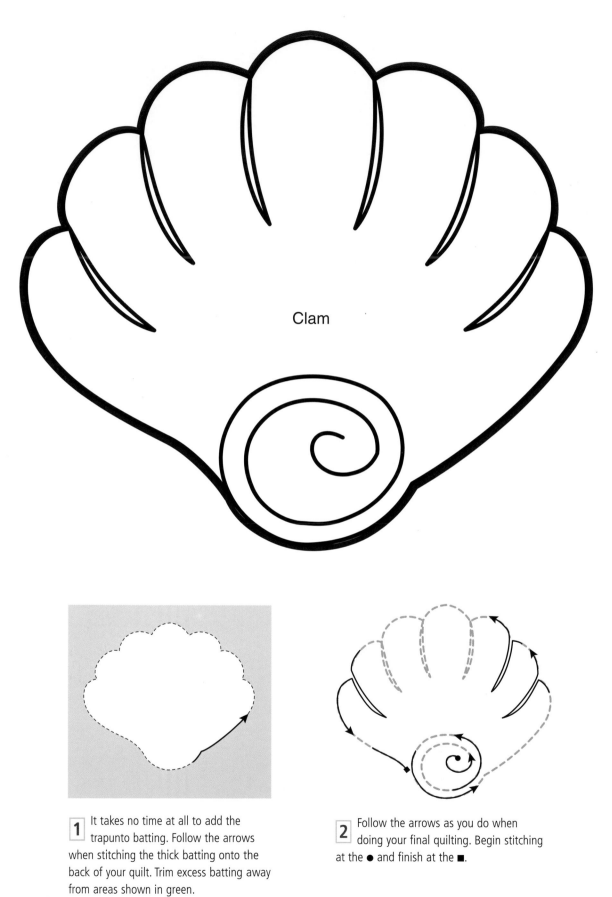

Clam

1 It takes no time at all to add the trapunto batting. Follow the arrows when stitching the thick batting onto the back of your quilt. Trim excess batting away from areas shown in green.

2 Follow the arrows as you do when doing your final quilting. Begin stitching at the ● and finish at the ■.

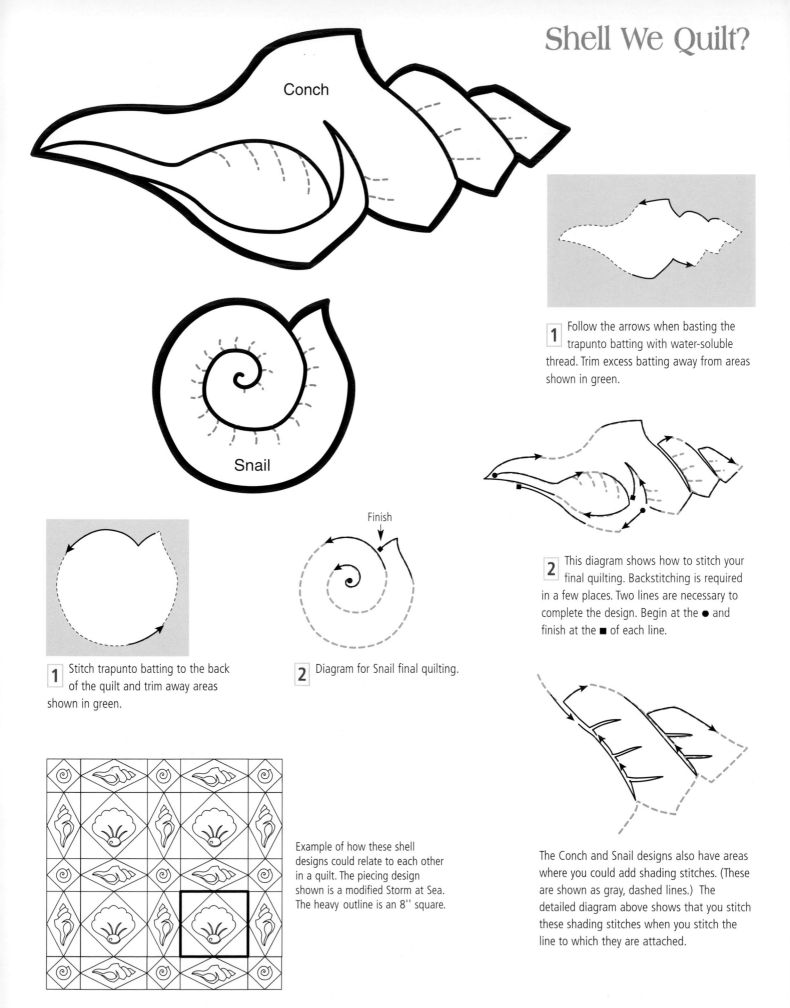

Conch

Snail

Finish

1 Follow the arrows when basting the trapunto batting with water-soluble thread. Trim excess batting away from areas shown in green.

2 This diagram shows how to stitch your final quilting. Backstitching is required in a few places. Two lines are necessary to complete the design. Begin at the ● and finish at the ■ of each line.

1 Stitch trapunto batting to the back of the quilt and trim away areas shown in green.

2 Diagram for Snail final quilting.

Example of how these shell designs could relate to each other in a quilt. The piecing design shown is a modified Storm at Sea. The heavy outline is an 8″ square.

The Conch and Snail designs also have areas where you could add shading stitches. (These are shown as gray, dashed lines.) The detailed diagram above shows that you stitch these shading stitches when you stitch the line to which they are attached.

Knot Crazy

This design is excellent for Cording Technique #1, pages 32-33.

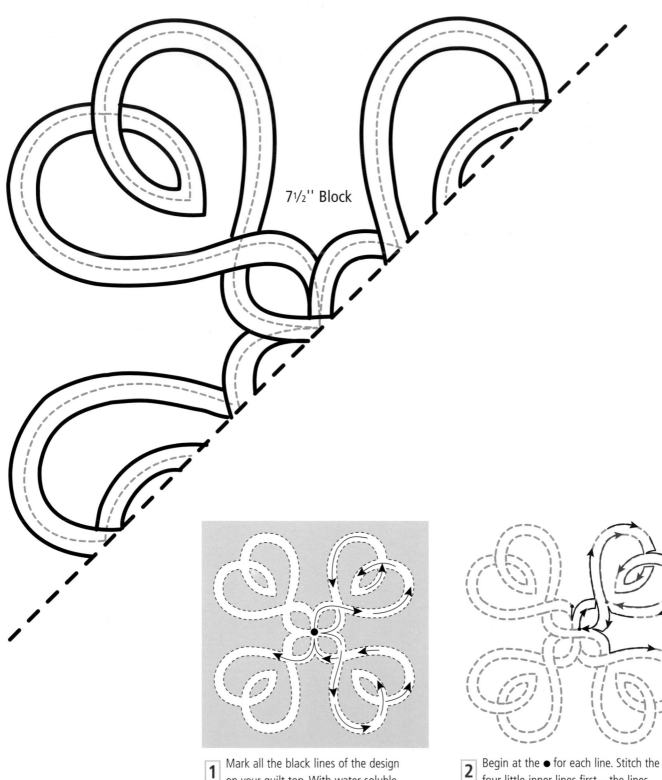

7½'' Block

1 Mark all the black lines of the design on your quilt top. With water-soluble basting thread, stitch down the center of the channels when basting the trapunto batting. Turn your quilt top over and trim away the batting a little more than ⅛'' on each side of the stitching. You will be trimming batting away from areas shown in green.

2 Begin at the ● for each line. Stitch the four little inner lines first—the lines that define the center of the hearts. The last line goes all the way around the design. It is actually a fun little puzzle.

Simplicity

See Hari's quilt on page 39.

5" Block

1½" Border

1 Stitch the outline with water-soluble thread, following the arrows. Trim excess trapunto batting away from areas shown in green.

2 Follow the arrows carefully to stitch Simplicity in one continuous line.

1 When stitching the trapunto batting on the back of your quilt top, stitch around the inner line first and then the outer line. Trim excess batting away.

2 Follow the arrows to stitch this border in a continuous line to stitch the final quilting.

Try reversing the direction of the motifs in the border for a different effect in the corners and in the centers of the borders.

Zenith

See Hari's quilt on page 4.

1 To make the pattern, trace half of Zenith onto each half of a piece of paper, as shown. Use a dark marker so the design will be easy to trace onto fabric.

Half of a 10'' Block

Remove a small amount of trapunto batting from between each design element for a sharper raised edge.

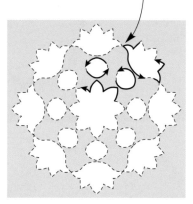

2 Follow the arrows when stitching the trapunto batting onto the back of your quilt top. Notice that the center, the circular shapes, and the flower heads are each stitched separately. This is so you can cut away a tiny amount of trapunto batting ($1/16''$–$1/8''$) from between each of them. This will give each element a sharper definition around its edge. Trim trapunto batting away from areas shown in green.

3 This design can be quilted in one continuous line. Begin stitching at the ● and carefully follow the arrows.

3½" Border

1 Follow the arrows to stitch the trapunto batting onto the back of the quilt top. The flowers are all stitched separately, as are the circular leaf motifs between the flowers. Line 1 and Line 2 are the connecting stem and the circular leaf motifs on the stem. This separate stitching allows you to cut a tiny amount of excess batting away from between the design shapes for a sharper final raised design. Trim excess batting away from areas shown in green.

Line 2
Line 1

2 The final quilting of the border is stitched in two lines. Line 1 is the bottom of the connecting stem and Line 2 is the top of the stem and the flowers and circular leaves.

Line 2
Line 1

Kansas

See Cheryl's quilts on page 44 and 45 and Cheryl's quilt on page 60.

See Cheryl's quilts on page 44 and 45 and Cheryl's quilt on page 60.

Place dashed line on fold of paper for tracing.

Half of a 10'' Block

This block is a nice hand quilting pattern because of minimal interior design lines.

1 Trace the Kansas design on each half of a sheet of folded paper.

2 Stitch the trapunto batting to the underside of your quilt top following the arrows. Trim excess batting away from areas shown in green. This diagram shows what a freezer paper stencil would look like.

3 Because of the inner areas of this design, you must quilt it in two lines. Begin at the ● and follow the arrows for each line.

3½'' Border

Border Repeat

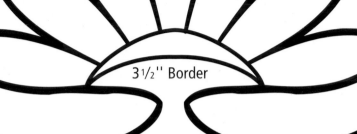

1 Stitch the trapunto batting to the back of your quilt top following these arrows. Line 1 is the simple inner line. Line 2 outlines the flowers. Trim excess batting away from areas shown in green.

Line 2
Line 1

2 The arrows guide you in stitching your final quilting. Line 1 is the simple inner line. Line 2 stitches the details in the flowers and completes the stem.

Line 2
Line 1

Ribbons and Bows

See Hari's quilt on page 44.
This design is also useful for reverse fake appliqué and tiny trapunto.

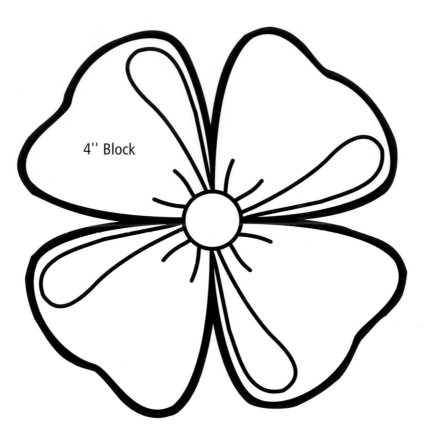

4" Block

If you want to stitch the shading lines, add them while you are stitching the line that includes the center of the bow and the line indicating the inside of the ribbon. See detailed drawing below.

1 Baste the thick trapunto batting with water-soluble thread, stitching just inside the outline of the bow. Trim excess batting away from areas shown in green.

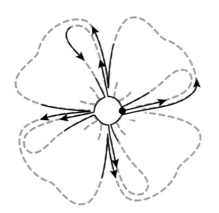

2 Begin at the ● and stitch the center and the inner lines first. When you get back to the ● go on to stitch the outer line. You will finish at the ●.

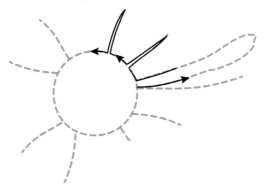

To make shading stitches as you are stitching the circle, take a few stitches and then stitch back over those stitches to get back to the circle again. It looks more complicated than it is. You can do it!

Ribbons and Bows

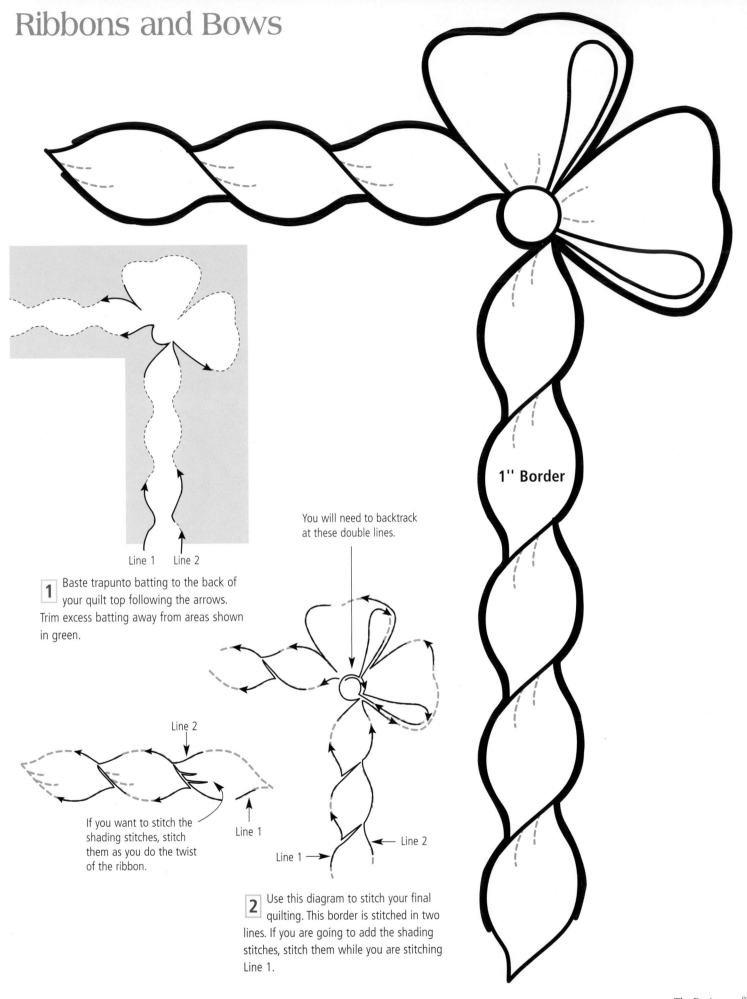

Line 1   Line 2

1 Baste trapunto batting to the back of your quilt top following the arrows. Trim excess batting away from areas shown in green.

You will need to backtrack at these double lines.

Line 2

If you want to stitch the shading stitches, stitch them as you do the twist of the ribbon.

Line 1

Line 1 →   ← Line 2

2 Use this diagram to stitch your final quilting. This border is stitched in two lines. If you are going to add the shading stitches, stitch them while you are stitching Line 1.

1'' Border

Splendid Susan

See Janet's quilt on page 48.

7" Block

Stitch the inside line first, then cross over the ● and stitch the outside line.

1 To baste the trapunto batting, begin at the ● and follow the arrows. Stitch the inside line first, then cross over at the ● and stitch the outer line. Trim excess batting away from area shown in green.

2 After your quilt sandwich is made, follow the arrows carefully and you will be able to stitch the entire design in one continuous line. Begin stitching at the ●

If you need a matching triangle, consider cutting this block on the diagonal. You will need to add a line to complete the half heart.

Splendid Susan

1½'' Border

Stitch the inner and outer outline with water-soluble thread as you add the thick trapunto batting. Trim excess batting away from the area shown in green.

1 Stitch the inner and outer outline with water-soluble thread as you add the thick trapunto batting. Trim excess batting away from the area shown in green.

2 It doesn't matter where you begin stitching, but you should follow the arrows carefully to stitch this design in one continuous line.

This design is lovely for fake appliqué.

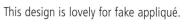

3½'' Block

1 Using water-soluble thread, follow the arrows to baste the thick trapunto batting. Trim excess batting away from the area shown in green.

2 Begin stitching at the ●. Follow the arrows carefully to stitch this design in one continuous line.

High Tide

See Jo's quilt on page 67.

If you leave the center of this design puffed, you can use the Cornerstone technique (pages 30-31) for a personalized initial.

7'' Block

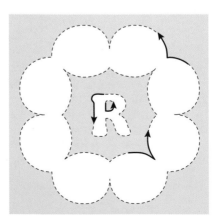

1 Stitch around the perimeter and inside lines with water-soluble basting thread as you add the thick trapunto batting. Trim excess batting away from areas shown in green.

If you want the center to remain "stuffed," only stitch the outside line with the water-soluble basting thread.

The letter R is shown only as an example for personalizing. See the alphabet on pages 92-93. The heart motif on the facing page is another option for this design.

2 Follow the arrows when doing your final quilting. It is something of an illusion, but the design is really stitched in one continuous line.

Add these lines at the corners.

2'' Border

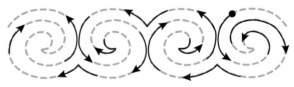

1 When adding the trapunto batting with water-soluble thread, you only need to stitch on the inner and outer lines. Trim excess batting away from areas shown in green.

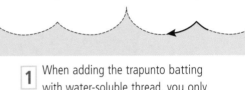

2 Follow the arrows as you do your final quilting. This border is stitched in one continuous line and you only need to stitch around your quilt once.

1 Follow the arrows to baste the trapunto batting. Trim excess batting away from the area shown in green.

2 The arrows show how to quilt this design in one continuous line as you do your final quilting. Begin at the ●.

2¹/4'' Heart

Border Repeat

See lettering and spacing tips in
Idea Two, Cornerstone Quilting
(page 31).

ABCD
EFGHI
JKLMN
OPQR
STUV
WXYZa

Entwined

See Sherri's quilt on page 68.

The peculiar shape of this design makes it very useful for blocks such as the Irish Chain family of piecing designs. These types of blocks often need a design that flows into the center side of the adjoining blocks.

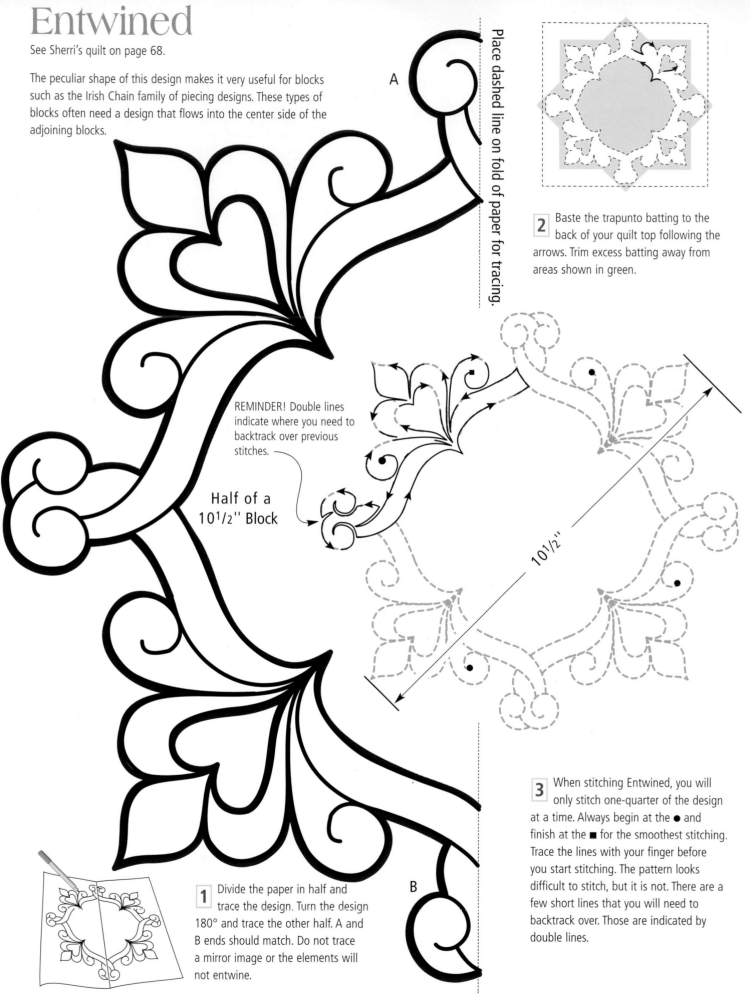

A

Place dashed line on fold of paper for tracing.

2 Baste the trapunto batting to the back of your quilt top following the arrows. Trim excess batting away from areas shown in green.

REMINDER! Double lines indicate where you need to backtrack over previous stitches.

Half of a 10¹⁄₂" Block

10¹⁄₂"

B

1 Divide the paper in half and trace the design. Turn the design 180° and trace the other half. A and B ends should match. Do not trace a mirror image or the elements will not entwine.

3 When stitching Entwined, you will only stitch one-quarter of the design at a time. Always begin at the ● and finish at the ■ for the smoothest stitching. Trace the lines with your finger before you start stitching. The pattern looks difficult to stitch, but it is not. There are a few short lines that you will need to backtrack over. Those are indicated by double lines.

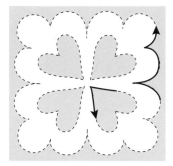

1 Follow this diagram to baste the trapunto batting to your quilt top. Trim excess batting away from areas shown in green.

2 Use this directional diagram as you do your final quilting. Each quarter section must be stitched separately. Begin at the ● and finish at the ■.

3¹/₂'' Block

This little 3¹/₂'' block is an ideal companion for the larger Entwined block. Below is a diagram showing how they look together.

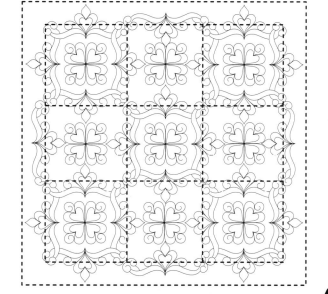

Suggestion for Whole Cloth Quilt

Mark your fabric in 7¹/₄'' squares. You need an uneven number of blocks in both directions. Mark a 3'' border allowance all the way around the outer edge of the fabric.

Center the large design in every other square, beginning with a corner square. This large block will overlap into the adjoining squares and the border allowance. Center the small block in the remaining squares. Line up the border section to the edge of the small blocks as shown to complete the border. Echo quilting would be a beautiful way to finish the background of this quilt.

Machine Quilted

See Hari's Quilt on page 12.

Detailed instructions are not given for this design. Many of the techniques given in this book could be used with this pattern.

Picture this design on a quilt for your sewing room or as a gift for a friend. You can trapunto the machine as shown on page 12, and/or you can add embellishments—large buttons and beads for knobs? If you add buttons, beads and other fun touches, add them after you do the quilting.

Although the needle area shown is quite detailed, you could simplify the shape and use this design as an appliqué pattern before you add the trapunto batting.

The electrical outlet appliqué pattern is useful for plugging your machine into the quilt border. It can either be AC or DC (current). You might get a charge out of this.

Vermont Leaves

See Margie's quilt on page 55.

These leaves can be corded with Cording Technique #1 (pages 32-33), or used with the Fake Appliqué technique. The following diagrams show how these leaves are trapuntoed with the Machine Trapunto technique.

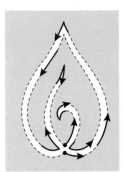

1 LEAF A. This is the guide for basting the trapunto batting. Trim excess batting away from green areas.

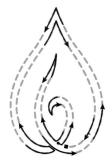

2 LEAF A. Follow the arrows for your final quilting. Begin at the ● and finish at the ■. You will backtrack over previous stitches where the double line is.

Leaf A

Leaf B

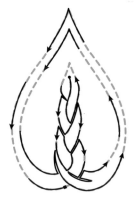

1 LEAF B. Follow this guide for basting the trapunto batting. Trim excess batting away from areas shown in green.

2 LEAF B. Follow the arrows when quilting. It is fun to stitch but you must backtrack over several short lines. Trace the path of the arrows with your finger first.

Sparkling Dahlia

See Maureen's quilt on page 59.

6" Block

Placed in an 8" square

1 The arrows show how to stitch the outline when you are stitching the trapunto batting for flower and leaves. Trim excess batting away from areas shown in green.

If you are making a stencil for reverse fake appliqué, the white shown would be the freezer paper.

2 FLOWER. Begin stitching at the ● and follow the arrows carefully to stitch Sparkling Dahlia in one continuous line.

3 LEAVES. Follow the arrows when doing your final quilting.

Set these leaf clusters side-by-side for a nice border.

Celebration Dancers

See Hari's quilt on page 102.

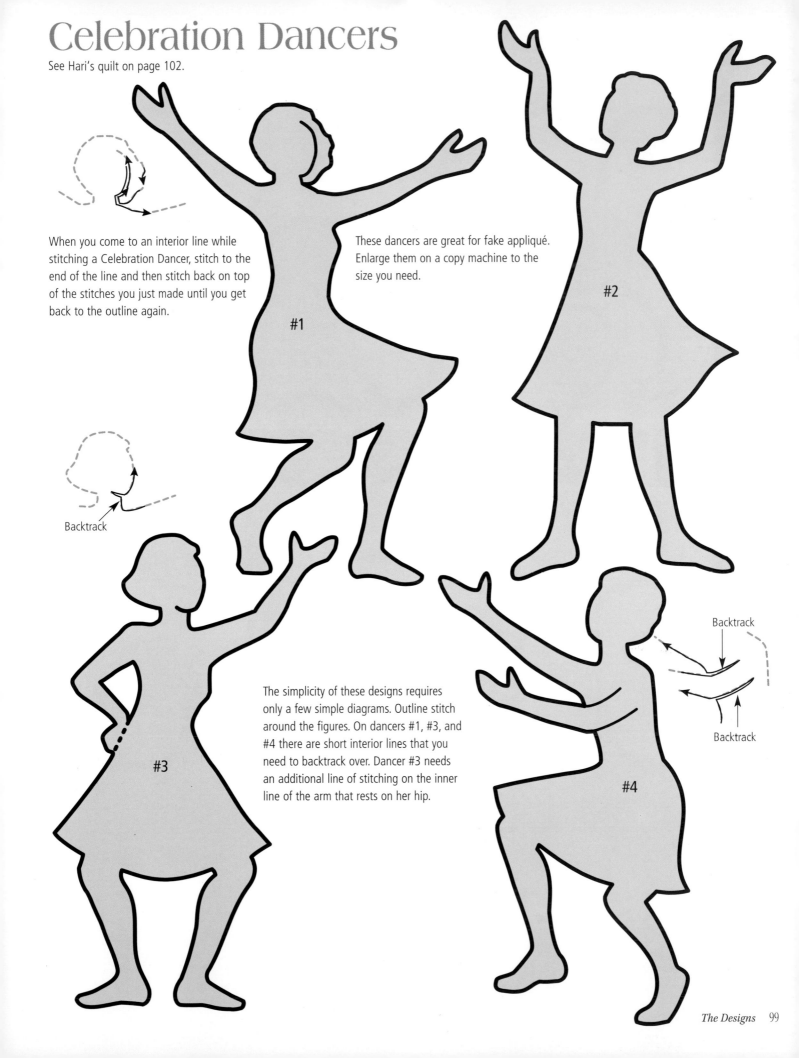

When you come to an interior line while stitching a Celebration Dancer, stitch to the end of the line and then stitch back on top of the stitches you just made until you get back to the outline again.

Backtrack

These dancers are great for fake appliqué. Enlarge them on a copy machine to the size you need.

#1

#2

#3

The simplicity of these designs requires only a few simple diagrams. Outline stitch around the figures. On dancers #1, #3, and #4 there are short interior lines that you need to backtrack over. Dancer #3 needs an additional line of stitching on the inner line of the arm that rests on her hip.

Backtrack

Backtrack

#4

7'' Block

1 Baste the trapunto batting with water-soluble basting thread following the arrows in the diagram on the left. Trim excess batting away from areas shown in green.

For reverse fake appliqué, the white would be the freezer paper stencil.

2 Follow the arrows in the diagram on the right to quilt this design in one continuous line. Begin stitching at the ● .

Paris

3" Border

3½" Block

Line 1

Line 2

1 When you are basting the trapunto batting for this border, stitch Line 1 first, all the way around your border. Then stitch Line 2. Trim excess batting away from areas shown in green.

2 Follow the arrows in this diagram when you are quilting the border. If you follow the lines of the design, it will be a continuous line and you will only need to travel once around your quilt border.

1 Stitch on the outlines as shown as you baste the trapunto batting. Trim excess trapunto batting away from areas shown in green.

2 Follow the arrows for your final quilting.

Reach Out, 47'' x 47''
Hari Walner

Too many times I have not had the courage to reach out and accept new adventures. When I first started thinking about using trapunto in non-traditional ways, this was one of the quilts I began to imagine. The figures are the Celebration Dancer designs on page 99 (and variations) using the Fake Appliqué technique shown in Idea Five (pages 39-41). The thick trapunto batting was added behind the light waves with regular thread, trimmed and then many different threads were used in the quilting. The dancers were also outlined with a dark quilting thread.

STAY OFF THE BEATEN PATH LONG ENOUGH AND YOU WILL BEAT A PATH

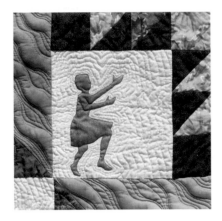

Traditions evolve for many reasons, not all of them good. Often they are a way for the elders of a society to organize and control a society. When a tradition no longer makes sense, or a better way supersedes it, the old tradition needs to be discarded. It doesn't make sense to blindly follow an old idea or method just because it is considered traditional. Good traditions constantly reinvent themselves on every part of our beautiful Earth.

We want to know and understand our history, to love and appreciate what folks were trying to say about their time. We are interested in their time on the planet. But, what are we saying about our time? Our today is ours, and it is very special in that it is the only bridge between yesterday and tomorrow.

When our children, grandchildren, and hopefully people several generations down the line look back at our lives and our works, let them be able to credit us with celebrating our own lives, and our own time.

Do not let ideas, just because they are "traditional" and old fashioned, get in the way of your art. When making a quilt, celebrate your time and your art.

You don't need to stay on the beaten path. Start your own traditions. You are the only you in this universe. Beat your own path.

Easy-Find Design Index

April, pages 71-72

Simplicity, page 81

April, pages 73-74

Zenith, pages 82-83

April, pages 75-76

Kansas, pages 84-85

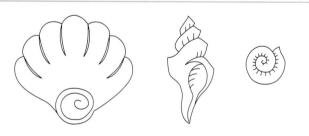

Shell We Quilt?, pages 78-79

Ribbons and Bows, pages 86-87

Knot Crazy, page 80

Splendid Susan, pages 88-89

High Tide, pages 90-91

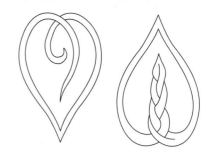

Vermont Leaves, page 97

ABCDEFGHIJ
KLMNOPQRS
TUVWXYZ
abcdefghijklm
nopqrstuvwxyz
1234567890

Alphabet, pages 92-93

Sparkling Dahlia, page 98

Entwined, pages 94-95

Celebration Dancers, page 99

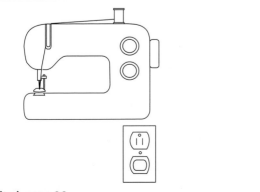

Machine Quilted, page 96

Paris, pages 100-101

THE QUILTERS

Approaching someone to make a quilt for a book is to ask them for their time, their creative energy, and their resources. The following quilters responded to my requests in many beautiful ways. I am in awe of their skills and feel privileged that they would share so much with us. What a lucky book!

BARBARA Totten

Although she is an experienced needleworker, Barb is new to the world of quiltmaking. After a career in the petroleum industry, Barb is now semi-retired and loves working in her garden. She plans to spend much of her time with a trowel in one hand and a needle in the other. Barbara's first quilt, *Midnight Star*, is on page 57.

CYNTHIA Catlin

Cynthia learned how to piece from her maternal grandparents, who were both prolific quilters. Because of career commitments, Cynthia and her family move often. This has allowed her broad exposure to many quilters and expanded her quiltmaking toolbox. Her quilt, *Essence of Friendship and Sisterhood*, is shown on page 64.

CHERYL Osborn

Cheryl loves to help children learn good eye-hand coordination by teaching them baton twirling. Her busy schedule of teaching and caring for her grandchildren does not leave much time for sewing, but she wanted to try hand quilting using this machine trapunto technique. *Just Do It*, her first hand-quilted quilt, is on page 60.

HANK Osborn

Hank's busy lifestyle includes working full time as an EMT specialist with an ambulance service and being a medical technician with the Wyoming National Guard. Precision piecing and free-wheeling machine quilting characterize his style and he finds quiltmaking a good opportunity to kick back and relieve pressures from his demanding work. Hank's quilt, *Calming the Waters*, is on page 56.

CHERYL Phillips

Cheryl is one of those art spirits whose creativity multiplies every year. She applies her originality to writing and teaching quiltmaking techniques. Her latest books, *Wedgeworks* and *Wedgeworks II*, are wonderful testaments to her unique approaches. She made several quilts for this book: including *The Healing Place*, page 47.

JANET Finley

Throughout her career as an executive secretary, Janet has developed a great sense of organization, which she has put to good use in her quiltmaking. She belongs to several quilting guilds, is president of the Columbine Guild in Wheatridge, Colorado, and is active with the American Quilt Study Group. Her quilt, *Loves Me, Loves Me Not*, is shown on page 48.

JERRY Nichols

Jerry began to quilt after she retired from a long career with AT&T in accounting/payroll. She is active in three quilt guilds: Adams County Quilters, Columbine Quilters, and the Colorado Quilting Council. Her beautiful precision quiltmaking skills and graceful machine quilting are evident in her quilt *Snowball Magic*, shown on page 50.

LESLIE Lott

Leslie's enthusiasm is infectious. You can't talk to her about quilts without feeling her energy. She loves to try new ideas and does so with gusto. Even working full time, Leslie finds time to enjoy her family and belong to both the Arapahoe County Quilters and the Colorado Quilting Council. Her quilt *Some of Life's Lessons* is on page 51.

JOSEPHINE Thogode

As busy as she is, she has hardly any quilts—Jo makes them all as gifts. The ideas keep entering her head, the thread keeps entering her needle, and her foot keeps the pressure on her machine pedal. Her quilt *Family Ties* on page 67, is one of the many lovely creations she made for a member of her family.

LESSIE Osborn

Although Lessie pieces her quilts by machine, she loves to hand quilt. Lessie was one of eighteen children, and her mother and aunt made sure she learned quilting skills at an early age. Her quilt *Country Woman* is on page 65.

JOSIE McKissick

After a career in office management, Josie turned to less stressful employment so she would have more time for grandchildren and quiltmaking. She manages it all, along with active membership in several quilt guilds, including the Colorado Quilting Council and the Rocky Mountain Wa Shonaji Quilt Guild. The two quilts Josie made for this book are *Nefer Again* and *Fancy That!*, shown on pages 54 and 61.

LINDA Taylor

Linda is the owner of Linda's Electric Quilters in McKinney, Texas. Her reputation as a pioneer in elegant heirloom quilting on industrial machines is growing rapidly, and her custom quilting is in constant demand. She has developed many innovative techniques, which she graciously shares with legions of students. The quilt Linda quilted for this book, *Paris*, is on page 26.

JULIA Payne

Julia is a story quilter. She approaches her work as a painter paints on canvas, using fabric as her medium, unhampered by quiltmaking rules. Her excellent sewing skills and a fertile imagination come together to produce her quilt art. Julia is an active member of both the Rocky Mountain Wa Shonaji Quilt Guild and the Colorado Quilting Council. Her quilt *Autumn Leaves* is shown on page 63.

LORAINE Kendrick-Gray

Loraine is the grandmother of twin girls with another set of twins on the way—plenty of inspiration to make quilts. She fills her home with lovely antiques and old quilts, but her own quiltmaking honors family members and tells stories. Loraine is a member of the Arapahoe County Quilters, Colorado Quilting Council, and the Rocky Mountain Wa Shonaji Quilt Guild. Her quilt *Anchors Away* is on page 66.

LYNETTE Bentley Fulton

Lynette never lacks for something to do. She is a Bernina® instructor, registered nurse, and machine quilting teacher, and also gives lectures to quilt guilds. She says quilting has enriched her life in many special ways, especially by the gift of dear friends. Her supportive husband Richard, is a retired firefighter, and a good cook too. Lynette's quilt *California Snowflake* is on page 49.

SHERRI Bain Driver

Sherri's teaching skills have a well-deserved enthusiastic following that is growing every day. She designs her own quilts, is always open to new construction methods, and practices excellent craftsmanship. She is a member of the Arapahoe County Quilt Guild and the Colorado Quilting Council. Her quilt *Half Past Autumn* is shown on page 68.

MARGIE Evans

Margie's business, Me Sew, Inc., keeps her busy, but never too busy to quilt or root around in out-of-the-way shops for beads and embellishments, paints, and beautiful threads. New ideas are never scary for Margie, who is one of those very creative California quilters. She used several of her favorite fabrics, techniques, and beads in her quilt, *Where the Wild Flowers Grow* on page 55.

SHIRLEY Wegert

Due to her phenomenal piecing skills, Shirley is one of the most prolific quilters in all of quiltdom. She is an excellent hand quilter as well as machine quilter. She has also sewn numerous quilts for Leman Publications, and loves to spend time with her many grandchildren. Her quilt *Honey Bee* is on page 62.

MAUREEN Newman

Maureen loves to travel—any excuse will do for a trip. Wherever she goes, she always investigates local needlework and picks up new inspiration. Although she didn't start sewing until 1991, she has been making up for lost time ever since, constantly trying new patterns and techniques. Maureen took time from her busy schedule to make *Flower Boxes*, shown on page 59.

SUE Danielson

Sue brought her superb dressmaking skills to quiltmaking in 1987. Although she is not a full-time quilter (her days are filled with her work as a molecular biologist) she has become a machine quilter par excellence, winning several top awards on a national level. The exquisite quilt she made for this book, *Renaissance*, appears on pages 52 and 53.

RAMONA Hilton

Mona enjoys decorating her home to give it a warm, loving, family atmosphere and making quilts adds to that warmth. During the day she is a nanny, which allows her to further share her giving nature. Although taking care of family and grandchildren also fills her busy days, she still found time to make *Passing Ships*, on page 58.

SOURCES

Alice Wilhoit
Classes in hand appliqué
9017 Conway Road
Anna, TX 75409
Ph: 972-924-2124
email: wwilhoit@earthlink.net

Beautiful Publications, LLC, publishers of
ContinuousLine® quilting patterns by Hari Walner
7508 Paul Place
Loveland, CO 80537-8732
Ph: 970-662-9950 (wholesale only)

Clotilde, mail-order source for
Wash Away basting thread, SoluThread, denim and embroidery machine needles, Hobbs batting, and fabric adhesive sprays
Ph: 800-772-2891

Creative Stitches, distributors of
DMC Machine Embroidery thread
230 W. 1700 South
Salt Lake City, UT 84115
Ph: 800-748-5144
www.creativestitches.com

Fairfield Processing, manufacturers of
Soft Touch, Cotton Classic and Hi-Loft Polyester Batting
P.O. Box 1130MJ
Danbury, CT 06813-1130
www.poly-fil.com

Hobbs Bonded Fibers, manufacturers of
Heirloom Cotton and Organic cotton batting
P.O. Box 3000
Mexia, TX 76667
Ph: 254-741-0041 (wholesale only)
Fax: 817-772-7238

Linda's Electric Quilters, dealer and classes for
long-arm quilting machines
215 E. Louisiana
McKinney, TX 96059
Ph: 800-893-2748
Fax: 972-542-4684
email: LEQuilters@aol.com

Janome America, Inc., distributors of
Janome Sewing Machines
10 Industrial Avenue
Mahwah, NJ 07430
website: www.janome.com

RJR Fashion Fabrics, finishers of
Quilter's sateen
13748 S. Gramercy Pl.
Gardena, CA 90249
Ph: 800-422-5426 (wholesale only)
website: www.rjrfabrics.com

Robert Kaufman Fabrics, finishers of
Ultra Sateen cotton
129 W. 132nd Street
Los Angeles, CA 90059-0266
Ph: 800-877-2066 (wholesale only)

Superior Threads, Inc., distributors of
SoluThread and SoluThread Extra, water-soluble basting thread.
PO Box 1672
St. George, UT 84771
Ph: 800-499-1777
e-mail: info@superiorthreads.com
website: www.superiorthreads.com

Stearns Technical Textiles Company, manufacturers of
Cotton Choice Batting and *Fat Batt*
100 Williams Street
Cincinnati, OH 45215-4683
Ph: 800-345-7150

YLI Corporation, distributors of
Wash Away water-soluble basting thread
161 W. Main Street
Rock Hill, SC 29730
Ph: 803-985-3100
Fax: 803-985-3106

BIBLIOGRAPHY

Sally Collins. *Small Scale Quiltmaking*, Martinez, CA: C&T Publishing, Inc., 1996.

Harriet Hargrave. *Mastering Machine Appliqué*, Martinez, CA: C&T Publishing, Inc., 1991.

Mary Mashuta. *Stripes in Quilts*, Martinez, CA: C&T Publishing, Inc., 1996.

Hari Walner. *Trapunto by Machine*, Martinez, CA: C&T Publishing, Inc., 1996.

Traditional Quiltworks 4th Annual Christmas Special. Montrose, PA: Chitra Publications, Inc., 1993.

Elly Sienkiewicz. *Appliqué 12 Easy Ways!,* Martinez, CA: C&T Publishing, Inc., 1991.

INDEX

Also by
Hari Walner

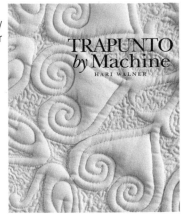

Other Fine Books From C&T Publishing

For more information write
for a free catalog:

C&T Publishing, Inc.
P.O. Box 1456
Lafayette, CA 94549
(800) 284-1114
http://www.ctpub.com
e-mail: ctinfo@ctpub.com

For quilting supplies:

Cotton Patch Mail Order
3405 Hall Lane, Dept. CTB
Lafayette, CA 94549
(800) 835-4418
(925) 283-7883
http://www.quiltusa.com
e-mail: cottonpa@aol.com

ABOUT THE AUTHOR

After a career in commercial and technical illustration and teaching painting and drawing, Hari began welding her life to quilts in 1987.

Her first book *Trapunto by Machine* was published by C&T Publishing in 1996. She designs *ContinuousLine*® quilting patterns for her business, Beautiful Publications, LLC, which she co-founded in 1990 with partner/husband Gordon Snow. At their home and workshop near Loveland, Colorado, they enjoy a view of the Rocky Mountain Front Range and share a fence with their neighbor's beautiful Texas Longhorn cattle. Together they love three adult children and four of the most wonderful grandchildren in the world.

"I am very happy to be able to design, quilt, and teach. These activities are rewards in themselves. To me, it is not important to be the best in anything. It is only important that I try my best: to give each design the time needed to develop into an idea that may inspire others to reach out, to share tips and techniques with quilters and hope they will realize their own uniqueness and carry on with confidence to swim into their own uncharted waters."